SOLOMON'S TOUCH

The life and work of Solomon J. Wickey

by

June Naugle

authorHOUSE™

1663 LIBERTY DRIVE, SUITE 200
BLOOMINGTON, INDIANA 47403
(800) 839-8640
WWW.AUTHORHOUSE.COM

First published by AuthorHouse 08/15/05

ISBN: 1-4208-5008-3 (sc)

Library of Congress Control Number: 2005904011

Printed in the United States of America
Bloomington, Indiana

This book is printed on acid-free paper.

Cover photo: Pat Centers and Stacey Crawford

**Dedicated to
Solomon's many loyal
friends and supporters**

FOREWORD

This book was never intended to be a scholarly work. It was intentionally written in a straightforward, unpretentious manner in keeping with the story.

It is based on the life and work of Solomon J. Wickey, a well-known Amish man who was falsely accused of practicing medicine without a license in the State of Indiana because he was a proficient iridologist and herbal nutritionist who sold herbs out of an office attached to a large barn on his farm, and gave hope and encouragement to thousands of people the established medical profession overlooked, or could not help.

As one of God's messengers with a special gift to heal, Solomon overcame all obstacles thrown in his way to develop a revolutionary new approach to health care; a simple "code" that will release and remove all manner of human ills instantly....no invasion, no drugs, no side effects, and it is FREE.

My research included searching through newspapers, letters and court documents, along with interviewing eyewitnesses in six states; English, Amish, businesspeople, professionals, students, and many whose lives were saved, or improved. It is as accurate as documentation and collective memory allows.

Solomon says, "When God wants you to do something, He makes a way for it to happen." Thus, I was "guided" to a company in the western United States where copies of all of the documents from his court trial were found tucked into a file cabinet after the originals had mysteriously disappeared from both the Adams

County courthouse, and the Indiana Attorney General's office in Indianapolis.

I am honored to write about this wonderful man whose work and reputation is known throughout the world. Hopefully, I've been able to bring to you, the reader, some of the more intimate, joyful and personal aspects of his life.

My sincere gratitude goes out to all of those too numerous to mention in this space, who so graciously helped in my effort to put this story on paper.

June Naugle

ONE

Sunday, February 27, 1938

The quiet peacefulness of pre-dawn was shattered by a sudden burst of squalling as Jacob and Elizabeth Wickey's sixth child, a son, announced his arrival. They named their precious new son Solomon after his grandfather, and Jacob after his father. Solomon Jacob Wickey.

Earlier, on the pretense of tending to his livestock on this cold, cloudy winter morning, Jacob had gone to the barn. Actually it was only an excuse. Truth be known, he felt useless, and was much too nervous to stay in the house waiting; just waiting. Besides, experience taught that the midwife had everything under control.

His farm was located two miles north of Berne, Indiana, surrounded by land owned by other farmers, who like himself, were members in good standing of the Old Order Amish community. The Wickey family was well-rooted there. Jacob, himself, was born in this same farmhouse. His parents were among several Old Order Amish families who had moved from Nappanee in Elkhart County, Indiana, to establish a new community in Adams County where rich, fertile land was available, and where they could live in harmony

1

according to the strict literal interpretation of the New Testament handed down by their ancestors.

It was not unusual for Old Order Amish families to relocate when their beliefs were threatened by a more liberal interpretation of the Scriptures. Old Order Amish adhere strictly to the interpretation, observance, and enforcement of the doctrine set forth by Anabaptist Jakob Ammann in Bern, Switzerland about 1690. He believed, and taught, that church is community, and from each of his followers he demanded purity in their lives and affairs, and the faithful practice of the discipline Jesus outlined in Matthew: 18.

After Jacob Wickey's first wife died, leaving him with three young daughters to raise, he married Elizabeth Wengert from Holmes County, Ohio, and together they had eight children, five boys, three girls; eleven children in all.

Carrying a glowing lantern, one of the older girls hurried to the barn to tell Jacob his son had been born.

Excited, he ran to the house ahead of her, bounded up the stairs to the bedroom he shared with Elizabeth, took his wife's small hand in his own, bent to kiss her, and whispered in her ear before he picked up the baby lying beside her.

Jacob Wickey was a kind, gentle, religious man, although at times, very stern. He cherished Elizabeth, as he did each of his children, considering them all to be gifts from God. After breakfast that morning, he bundled the older children into the family buggy for the trip to church, where he served as minister.

News of baby Solomon's arrival had spread quickly throughout the Amish community, so naturally, the men in his church district greeted him with congratulating handshakes and playful slaps on the back. The local newspaper, **The Berne Witness**, printed the birth announcement on the front page the next day.

Solomon was a happy, contented baby with bright blue eyes and fluffy tufts of dark hair, but from the first moment she held him in her arms, Elizabeth Wickey knew there was something that set this child apart from her other children. He was different; different in a way she couldn't explain, nor did she try. She just knew. And because of that knowingness, an unusual bond developed between the two of them which remained strong as long as she lived.

Solomon adored his sister, Rebecca, who, being only fifteen months older than he, was still a baby herself. They became inseparable playmates, entertaining themselves with homemade toys, or whatever happened to be at hand; wooden spoons, blocks, clothespins, a ball of string, the farm dog, or a barn cat if they could catch one. In their baby talk she called him Solly, he called her Becky...names they affectionately kept for each other even as adults.

Elizabeth's great love of horses was a passion she passed on to Solomon. It was not unusual for her to balance him on her hip with Rebecca toddling alongside, as she took them to the barnyard to play with a horse hitched there. So excited was he, that Solomon would try to wiggle out of her arms in his eagerness to run his pudgy little fingers along the big muscular neck, or grab a tiny fistful of straggly mane. He tingled with excitement when she hoisted him atop the horse then picked up Rebecca to sit behind him. Perfectly happy and contented, he sat erect, giggling and clucking as if he'd been riding for years. But, oh, the shrill shrieks he let out when she lifted him down and headed back to the house.

Solomon's most prized possession as a child was a rocking horse his dad and older brother, Amos, made for him from a nail keg. He rode that little keg steed long after his feet touched the ground; until it dropped dead when the slats loosened, separated and fell apart under his weight.

Solomon owned many beautiful horses throughout the years, but none as prized, or more memorable, than that little keg horse that could trot or gallop upon demand. Many young children are fearful and have to be coaxed into touching something as big and scary as a horse, but not Solomon. Horses seemed to understand his love for them because Jacob's huge draft horses stood perfectly still as he squirmed around under their bellies before he was yet two years old, hugging their legs and pulling their tails. However, they stomped, snorted, and impatiently flipped their long tails when other children came near. Elizabeth was convinced that his life-long romance with horses began in the womb. Perhaps she was right.

For young Solomon, life revolved around his mother, Rebecca, horses, and of course, church. Even before he could speak clearly he followed his mother wherever she went, asking one question after another about verses of Scripture he'd heard read in church. His understanding of the Bible, as well as his unending stream of questions, vexed her. He seemed to know things about the Bible she couldn't explain, and any attempt to do so was feeble to say the least. This child was definitely a challenge.

In 1943 Old Order Amish parochial school had not yet been established in Adams County, so according to the law, Amish children were required to attend public school. Rebecca was born in November, and since children entering first grade had to be six years old on the first day of school, she couldn't attend the Spunger School until the following September, a rule that pleased Solomon immensely. But all too soon the dreaded day came when the school bus forced them apart.

4

This, their first separation, was painful for both children, particularly for Solomon. He wandered around day after day, followed by an old lop-eared dog, not knowing what to do without her. He had two younger brothers, but they were too little to do the things he wanted to do. He wanted to play with Becky. She could run fast, and wasn't afraid to climb the ladder to the hayloft, or roll around in the hay stored there, and she knew all the secret places where the setting hens laid their eggs, and she loved to scatter cracked corn around the barnyard for chicken scratch, and she wasn't afraid of the new colts or calves, and she could crawl under the corncrib to discover where the cat hid her new kittens. Important things! Things they could do just as soon as the awful old school bus brought her back home.

By winter Solomon was beginning to adjust to the routine public education had forced upon him, but suddenly his young life was shattered when his beloved Becky, his precious playmate, was stricken with Polio. Childhood ended abruptly. She was seven years old; he was five.

TWO

Polio. It was the only topic of conversation throughout the Amish community, or so it seemed to a little boy not yet six years old. From the worried look on adult faces and the tone of their voices when they talked about it, Solomon knew polio was something very serious, but he had absolutely no understanding of just how serious.

His mother tried to explain to him that Rebecca had contracted a terrible disease and was quarantined in the isolation ward at Lutheran Hospital in Ft. Wayne, which, to a child who rarely left his own yard, seemed a million miles away.

Solomon missed his sister terribly. He cried constantly. Elizabeth cuddled him on her lap whispering to him as gently as she could that Rebecca was much too sick to come home right then, nor could he go see her, although she, herself, spent as much time with her daughter trying to calm her fears as the hospital staff would allow. Rebecca was terrified to be left alone in that strange place with other children, all of whom were rendered helpless, didn't know what was happening to them, and screamed to go home. Most of them were delirious from high fever, couldn't move their legs, and were scared to death. Rebecca was even more frightened because she couldn't speak, nor understand, the language. Only the Swiss-

7

German dialect of their Old Order Amish ancestors was spoken in the Wickey home, and she had not yet learned to speak English at school.

Jacob Wickey stroked his long, thin beard incessantly out of habit as he always did when he took a personal problem to God. He and Elizabeth were worried sick about Rebecca; about all of their children, in fact, especially about Solomon, Rebecca's constant shadow. Poliomyelitis, more commonly referred to as polio or infantile paralysis, was a mysterious, highly contagious disease without a known cure in 1943, a terrifying epidemic that swept across the United States killing thousands of victims and crippling others, mostly children. Jacob's and Elizabeth's prayers were answered. The rest of their children were spared.

Rebecca was a brave, plucky little girl even when her doctors said there was little, if any, hope that she would ever walk again. Sister Elizabeth Kenny, a dedicated nurse from Australia, arrived in the United States in the early 1940s to challenge traditional methods of treating paralytic polio. Instead of the orthodox treatment most U.S. doctors prescribed for total bed rest to immobilize the affected limbs, Sister Kenny (her title *Sister* was the British term for nurse) advocated hot, moist packs applied to painful muscles two or three times every day, followed immediately by a warm bath, then an icy spray to stimulate circulation. Between the hot Kenny Pack treatments, therapists massaged the children, and along with range-of-motion exercise, moved limbs and muscles that were paralyzed.

The doctors at Lutheran Hospital followed Sister Kenny's treatment method to the letter. During the nineteen long months she was in the hospital, Rebecca grew accustomed to extremely hot cotton flannel, or thick, wet, itchy wool rags being placed on her body morning, noon, and night, followed by painfully intense physical therapy on her motionless legs. Elizabeth continued the hot Kenny Pack treatments for many months after Rebecca came home, with Solomon standing beside her bed observing every detail, always begging to help. It was his first experience with disease, but by no means his last.

Solomon's horizons broadened considerably that fall when he entered first grade at the two-room Spunger School only a couple of miles down the road. He was a good student and with the help of a teacher who was fluent in the Swiss-German dialect spoken by local Amish families, quickly learned to write and speak English. But, for him, the highlight of each day was rushing home to take care of Rebecca.

Jacob, a carpenter by trade, made a small child-sized wheelchair for his young daughter. It had oversized wheels making it easy even for a little boy to push, and when she felt well enough Solomon took her with him everywhere he went. Never were two children happier to be together. On warm sunny days they played outside as before. Sometimes he rolled her under the shade of a big tree while he sat on a limb above watching over her as he recited aloud verses of Scripture he had memorized. They took exciting, adventure-filled trips down the lane to the mailbox, or to the barnyard filled with wondrous places to explore.

Rebecca Wickey was a very pretty little girl with flawlessly smooth skin and beautiful bright eyes. She was also very smart. During the next few years she was in and out of the hospital several times, but when she was well enough, the Adams County school administration sent teachers to the house to home-school her. She loved her lessons, learned quickly, and tried her best to catch up with Solomon.

Solomon enjoyed school too, but preferred the warm, sunny days of summer, which he spent gardening, farming, tending to the horses, doing whatever chores he was assigned, and of course, spending time with Rebecca. But come September he cheerfully boarded the school bus, ready for another year filled with rich new learning experiences.

He attended Spunger School through fifth grade, and went to Monroe Elementary for sixth, seventh and eighth grades. The new Adams County High School was still under construction at the beginning of Solomon's freshman year so he went to Kirkland High School for a few weeks before transferring to the new high school as soon as it was completed. He finished his formal schooling there, excelling in industrial arts.

School did not interfere with things going on at home. Solomon loved gardening. Sometimes when she felt up to it and weather permitted, Rebecca sat at the edge of the garden so they could talk, or sing, while he painstakingly planted, hoed and weeded. He grew a wide variety of vegetables and a few kitchen herbs, and took great pride in always having a perfect, weed-free garden. When the vegetables were ready to harvest, he pulled radishes, tender green onions, carrots, beets, tomatoes, and shucked luscious ears of tender sweet corn. He and Rebecca made a game of shelling peas and snapping green beans under "their tree." Elizabeth and his older sisters planned meals around whatever Solomon harvested that day. His garden always produced enough to can for winter meals, too.

Even before Solomon became a teenager, his quiet, compassionate personality had become clearly defined. He allowed Rebecca, and sometimes Elizabeth, into his private thoughts, but few others. His brothers and sisters made little, if any, effort to understand his sensitive, caring ways, nor did they pay him any attention at all. They treated him cruelly, told their friends that he was different and eccentric; somewhat a laughing stock who just didn't fit in. It was little wonder they didn't like him, or understand him; they hardly knew him.

Among Old Order Amish families, the church has always been the core of their strong cohesive bond. It influences every aspect of their lives, is the origin of news, as well as community and social activities. The Wickey children attended church regularly, made friends, and enjoyed a normal social life...all of them except Solomon and Rebecca, that is. Church clothes were not provided for either of them, because during the many months Rebecca was not strong enough to leave home neither of them went to church, nor anyplace else for that matter.

Actually, Solomon found joy in staying at home with Rebecca while the rest of the family went to church. They sang songs from the Ausbund, the official Swiss-German hymnal, took turns reading Scriptures, and strengthened their bond by having a private worship service at home, just the two of them.

Solomon's siblings were very envious of his many natural talents. Much to their chagrin, he was light-years ahead of all of them when it came to drawing, singing, yodeling. When he drew a picture of a horse it looked like a horse down to the last detail, while their feeble attempts were nothing more than clumsy, disjointed lines that had no resemblance, whatsoever, to good horseflesh. An example of his early art work, in the form of a pencil drawing, still remains in good condition just inside the main door in the barn on the Wickey home place.

The teen years brought new interests, new challenges, for both Solomon, and Rebecca. She blossomed into a lovely young woman, he searched for a whisker or two on his chin.

Solomon developed into a handsome young man with penetrating blue eyes and a head full of thick dark hair. His body was skinny, but the muscles in his chest, arms and shoulders were unusually strong and well-developed from carrying Rebecca everywhere. His legs were thin, but **very strong**. Not only could he run fast, he could also stand flat on the ground, grab the barbed wire in one hand and jump over a four-foot wire fence from a standing position.

One of the most significant events in Solomon's life was learning to shoot a gun. Regardless of work, or other responsibilities, he always found time for target practice and hunting, either alone, or with a friend. He became an expert marksman.

Solomon's brothers couldn't begin to match his marksmanship, strength or agility. To mask their envy, some of them...particularly the one who held a life-long grudge against Solomon...constantly berated him, told him he was ignorant, a real loser that would never amount to anything because he acted different than other Amish boys, he was weird, he couldn't do anything right, and a host of other hateful, derogatory remarks that were hurtful. Instead of responding, Solomon just licked the emotional wounds they inflicted upon him, and stayed out of their way.

Rebecca's improved health encouraged an interest in a social life which, of course, revolved around church activities. She thrived on the company of other girls her age; the giggles, the gossip, the secrets, even occasional glances at boys. Her parents spoiled her terribly, giving her everything she wanted upon demand.

When his older brothers began to marry and leave home, Solomon took on a greater share of the farm work. There was always something to be done. When he wasn't in school, he worked long hours alongside his dad as a carpenter's apprentice. Jacob Wickey was also a fine blacksmith. On days they didn't have construction work he and his sons shoed their own horses, as well as those from around the neighborhood, sharpened plow points, and sometimes forged new parts for well-used machinery.

As soon as the weather dipped below freezing in the fall or early winter, the Wickeys butchered enough hogs to provide meat for several weeks. The whole family pitched in to help. The boys killed, hung and drew each animal, but not one of them knew how to open a hog, or how to remove the entrails, even though in years past they had made clumsy attempts to cut up the carcass. Before he was fifteen years old, the task of butchering fell to Solomon. Nobody asked him if he thought he could do it. He was simply told it was his job.

Without hesitation, he sharpened a knife to a razor edge, and with the confidence of a brain surgeon skillfully wielding a scalpel, he made an incision and removed the entrails. He then carefully by-passed veins, separated tissue, and delicately removed the heart and liver…his first lesson in anatomy. His brothers pitched in to help trim out the hams, shoulders, sweetbreads, tenderloin, ribs and bacon, or slab meat as they called it.

The men ground the scraps into sausage, and rendered lard in huge iron kettles over an open fire. By day's end all of the hams, shoulders, and slabs of bacon had been sugar cured and carefully hung in the smokehouse.

The women sewed long muslin casings which they filled with fresh sausage that had been seasoned with sage, salt and pepper, then sealed with a thick layer of melted fat and hung in the smokehouse alongside the hams, shoulders and bacon. Nothing was wasted. The feet, tongues, and tails were pickled, the rest was canned.

Solomon's teenage years were relatively happy.   Jacob bought a new horse, a mixed Standardbred and Quarterhorse gelding standing about fifteen hands tall that had been broken to the saddle, as well as to the buggy.   His sons were thrilled because, theretofore, they'd had only big, broad draft horses which were definitely not suitable for riding.   Brother Jake trained the new horse to neck-rein, while Solomon took charge of its daily care.   He lovingly hugged the animal, scratched its ears, and gently stroked every inch of its body as he brushed and curried.   All the while, he spoke softly, soothingly, to acquaint the horse with not only his smell, but his voice as well.

Every Sunday evening Solomon hitched the new horse to a two-seated open buggy, carefully lifted Rebecca onto the front seat, settled her wheelchair in the back, and away they went to *the singing*, the weekly social gathering of the young single people in their church district.   Sunday evening singings were held in the home of whoever hosted church earlier in the day.   (Old Order Amish church is always held in one of the members' house or barn).   A cafeteria-type meal was provided for the young folks; boys ate on one side of a long table, girls on the other side.   Amish tradition prohibits them from sitting side by side.

Usually there was a short period of visiting and subtle flirting after the dishes were cleared.   Gradually some of the girls returned to sit at the long tables where they began singing softly; acappella, according to Amish custom.   Other girls joined in.   Presently, the boys took their places on the opposite side of the table and added their voices.

Many of the songs had the same words as those used at the morning church service, but were sung to different tunes and a faster tempo.   Solomon and Rebecca took great pleasure in harmonizing their beautiful singing voices in a duet at every Sunday evening singing.

Normally the singing ended about nine-thirty. While Rebecca lingered for a few minutes with her friends, Solomon hitched the new horse to the buggy and lighted the lanterns before they clippety-clopped toward home in the stillness of night.

THREE

It was at the Sunday evening singings that the romance between Rebecca and Joseph Girod began to blossom. They courted in the traditional way, for the traditional length of time, before they were married, and according to Amish custom lived at the home of the bride's parents as newlyweds. Joseph and Rebecca later built a house and established their own home right there on the Wickey home-place, where their three sons were born and raised.

Instead of being lonely when Rebecca got married, Solomon discovered that a whole new life existed out there beyond the farm, and did he ever take advantage of it. He worked every day as a finish carpenter, and for the first time in his life had good clothes to wear with money in his pocket. His only intention at the time was to make new friends and have FUN, FUN, FUN! The success of that mission surpassed even his wildest expectations.

In the course of events, Solomon attended the wedding of one of his friends who lived near Berne. Cupid shot an arrow into the air that day. On its way back to earth it struck Solomon in the heart when, across the room, he first spotted the smiling face of beautiful, petite Anna Mae Graber.

Anna Mae Graber. There was something very special about her, and even though they had not been properly introduced, Solomon liked the way her name echoed through his mind as he silently repeated it again and again. He sat erect, pretending to pay rapt attention to the bishop's wedding sermon, but actually, Anna Mae Graber stole his concentration that day.

In keeping with Amish custom, an hour or so before the evening meal was served it was the new bride's privilege to make a list of young couples that would sit together for supper, and also for the evening singing…the final event of the wedding celebration.

With notebook in hand the new bride mingled with the young, unmarried men, jotting down the name of the girl each chose. This was one of the few times couples who were going steady, or wanted to, were seen together in the presence of their parents. Without hesitation, Solomon gave Anna Mae's name. When she learned Solomon Wickey had chosen her for his supper partner she blushed with teenage delight. After all, his glances had not gone unnoticed.

When the older folks had finished eating it was time for the young people to assemble, boys in one room, girls in another. As the helper to whom the bride had given her list called out the names of each couple, the boy and girl came out, faced each other, joined hands, and together went to find their assigned places at the supper tables. It was an exciting moment!

After that most memorable evening almost a year passed before they saw each other again. Solomon was only eighteen years old when they met, too young to have a serious girlfriend. Besides, he didn't think having a special girlfriend was in his immediate future….but circumstances seem to have a way of changing.

A couple of months before his nineteenth birthday, Solomon attended another wedding, and much to his delight Anna Mae

18

Graber was also there. She looked even more beautiful than he remembered.

Several weeks after their second meeting arrangements were made for the older teenagers in Solomon's church district to travel to Grabill, Indiana for a singing. It was customary to go on Friday afternoon and return on Saturday afternoon. The days dragged by. Solomon thought Friday would never come. There was someone in Grabill he wanted to see.

Over the next several months, almost a year, in fact, Solomon and Anna Mae looked forward to every social gathering between their respective church districts. A romance was quietly beginning to flourish right under the watchful eye of church chaperons.

Solomon couldn't get the image of her face out of his mind. It seemed to be permanently etched there. Wherever he was, wherever he looked day or night, there she was smiling back at him. She stirred a longing in his heart, in his soul, and definitely in his mind. There was no doubt about it, he wanted to court this young woman. When he asked permission, she quickly agreed.

Solomon and Anna Mae were ready to get married right away even though Amish tradition would not permit such a hasty decision. They had been taught that both life and tradition are sacred. Honoring Amish tradition was important. They could wait.

Grabill is located about forty miles northeast of Berne. But to a young man falling in love, distance didn't matter.

In addition to tilling the soil, taking care of the horses and the garden, and doing a variety of other chores, Solomon continued to work for his dad's construction company. But around noon on Saturday, scrubbed clean and wearing his best, he started walking north on U.S. 27 with his thumb out to hitch a ride. He wasn't choosey. Whatever stopped; buggy, truck, automobile, he jumped in…just as long as it was headed toward Grabill. Unless weather interfered, he made the trip every week. Between visits he and Anna Mae kept the mailman busy delivering letters.

His intentions were clear from the very beginning. As far as her father was concerned, any young man willing to hitchhike eighty miles every weekend to court his daughter was a serious suitor.

Anna Mae's parents liked Solomon, and welcomed him into their family; a family with which he felt quite comfortable. When he was there he took meals with them, helped with the chores, stayed overnight in their home, went to church with them, and used Mr. Graber's horse and buggy for visits with Anna Mae's family or friends on Saturday night, and to the Sunday evening singings. However, well before the first crack of dawn on Monday morning, he was out on the road heading back to Berne. He had to be there in time to go to work.

This routine continued for a year-and-a-half. Amish courtships move slowly. Traditionally, courting lasts about six months before the more serious dating period of one year begins. Couples need time to get acquainted with each other, time to think and pray, time to allow genuine love and respect to grow. Among Old Order Amish, marriage is a lifetime commitment; nothing to rush into.

Solomon and Anna Mae chose Thursday, January 29, 1959, as the date for their wedding. It was the day before her twentieth birthday, and one month before this twenty-first. Earlier, Solomon had spoken to her father, telling him of their plans and asking permission to marry his daughter. Mr. Graber nodded his approval and gave the marriage his blessing.

Solomon was eager to get married. So much so, in fact, that he decided to get a head start on growing his beard. But his efforts were futile. No matter how much he tried, nothing happened. Nary a hair grew on his chin for six whole years; not until he was twenty-seven years old.

A few weeks prior to the wedding, Solomon made a trip to see the deacon in his own church district. He explained that he planned to marry Anna Mae Graber on January 29th, and asked for the blessing of the church. The deacon was well acquainted with Solomon. He knew him to be an Old Order Amish member in good standing, and agreed to accept his petition. He answered, to the satisfaction of the deacon, all of the questions required of a marriage petitioner, and took an oath swearing that he had remained pure.

It was the responsibility of his deacon to deliver the marriage petition to the deacon in her church district for approval. Once it was received, her deacon went to the Graber home to ask Anna Mae if it was true that she planned to marry Solomon Jacob Wickey on January 29th. She responded shyly, saying yes that was her intention. Then he solemnly asked if she could swear in front of God and her peers that she had remained pure? She looked him straight in the eye as she proudly answered, "Yes!" By proclaiming her innocence, she would be permitted to wear a white cape, white bonnet and white apron on her wedding day.

With the necessary preliminaries out of the way, the deacon sat down with Anna Mae and her parents to discuss wedding plans.

It would be a traditional Old Order Amish ceremony, of course, to be held in the bride's home, and conducted entirely in Swiss-German. The bishop, and two deacons, one from each of their church districts, would officiate. Solomon and Anna Mae had chosen to have a small, simple wedding with only two attendants each; his cousins, her sisters. The guest list would be limited to their families and close friends which, even so, numbered well over one-hundred-fifty people.

The Graber household became a beehive of activity almost immediately. As with any mother of the bride who is planning a wedding, Mrs. Graber made a long list of things to be done. The house had to be thoroughly cleaned from top to bottom. The menu for a bountiful noon meal and a light supper for all of the guests had to be planned. She would ask several relatives to cook and serve the food. Other relatives would be asked to set up the tables and benches, spread the tablecloths, and wash dishes. Mr. Graber was in charge of asking young teenage boy cousins to take care of unhitching the buggies, and others to feed and stable the guests' horses for the day.

Two weeks before their wedding, Solomon and Anna Mae went to the Allen County Courthouse in Ft. Wayne to apply for their marriage license, even though they had not yet been officially published. (*Published* is the term which refers to the deacon's announcement of an approaching marriage at the close of a regular Sunday church service. In this case he was late in doing so).

By four o'clock on Thursday morning, January 29, the Graber household was bustling with excitement. There was so much to be done before the wedding. The men folks headed to the barn to do the morning chores; milk cows, feed horses, hogs and cattle. The girls raced to the henhouse to feed and water the chickens and gather eggs. Mrs. Graber tidied the house and cooked a hearty breakfast for the bride and groom and their attendants, even though they all said they were too nervous to eat very much.

Buggies filled with guests and helpers, as well as several cars and vans bringing relatives from a distance, began arriving before dawn.

22

In keeping with Amish custom, the wedding began promptly at nine o'clock. As the guests sang a hymn from the Ausbund, one of the attendant couples joined hands and entered the room to start the wedding procession.

Solomon and Anna Mae, hands clasped firmly, walked slowly to their place of honor at the front of the room. He was handsome, and very confident, in his new black suit, white shirt, black bow tie. She looked radiant beside him in her white cape, white bonnet, and white apron worn over a lovely new black dress.

The wedding procession ended with the second attendant couple taking their places in front of the six identical chairs which had been placed in full view of both the bishop and the guests. Solomon and Anna Mae sat between their two attendants...he between his cousins, she between her sisters...the three women facing the three men.

The service began with the ministers offering lengthy prayers, followed by favorite Bible stories. Each of the deacons then read several passages of Scripture relating to the marriage covenant.

The bishop was the main speaker. His sermon, taken from I Corinthians and Ephesians, dealt with the commitment of marriage, and the appropriate relationship between a husband and wife. Then abruptly, while holding a German New Testament in his hand, he asked Solomon and Anna Mae to step forward to repeat their wedding vows. He pronounced them man and wife, blessed their union, and told them to go forth and live their lives together in the name of the Lord.

Without embracing, they returned to their respective seats and joined the guests as they kneeled in prayer. The church service closed with the guests singing the traditional Amish wedding hymn while the wedding party walked out.

It was noon. Everyone was hungry. As tables were set up and spread with snow white tablecloths, a gentle rain started to fall, but the guests who were occupied with eating and visiting, hardly noticed.

Late in the afternoon nature played a dirty trick. Suddenly, the temperature shot down without warning, then plunged even further. Before the men could harness their horses and hitch them to buggies for a quick departure, the rain turned to a glistening sheet of solid ice. All of the guests were forced to spend the night.

So much for the newlyweds' long anticipated honeymoon!

It is not good that man should be alone:
I will make him a helper.
Genesis 2:18

FOUR

Theirs was a blissful marriage from the very beginning. Solomon enjoyed living in the Amish community near Grabill where he and Anna Mae found joy in being together, surrounded by loving family and friends.

It is customary for Old Order Amish newlyweds to live with the bride's parents for a period of at least six months. Solomon and Anna Mae stayed longer; more than a year, in fact. They were happy and contented, and were simply in no hurry to move. Besides, it was important to take time to know each other as husband and wife; time to establish a solid foundation for a loving, life-long partnership before taking on the full responsibility of a home and family.

Almost immediately after the wedding, Solomon took a job as foreman with a local construction company. The hours were long, but he liked the work and the salary was good. He was determined to provide well for his wife and the children they would have. He wanted his children to have things he was deprived of when he was young, such as good shoes and clothes to wear to church. He was also eager to own land, a home, horses, cattle, and he was willing to work hard to obtain these things, and more.

By summer Anna Mae was pregnant with their first child, and Solomon began thinking about a home for his precious little family. He and Anna Mae decided to accept her parent's generous offer of a building site located on Graber land across the road from their own home.

In his spare time during the next several months, and with the help of Mr. Graber, Solomon dug and finished the basement where they planned to live temporarily until they could complete the house. In the fall of 1960, Solomon, Anna Mae, and baby David moved into their new basement home. Life was good!

Hoofs and wheels are a young Amish man's pride and joy, just as a shiny new motorized vehicle is to other young men. To satisfy his inherent love for hoses, as well as his young-man ego, Solomon bought a sleek, black, registered Standardbred gelding to hitch to his buggy, and oh, was he ever proud!

Later, he bought a registered Standardbred mare for the purpose of starting a small herd. He knew the demand for registered Standrardbreds to pull fast moving Amish buggies would make the venture profitable.

The Standardbred is the world's fastest horse under harness, working either as a trotter or pacer. While the Thoroughbred, the other race horse, traces its ancestory to English pedigrees bestowed upon four superior stallions that serviced the royal mares ensconced in the king's stables in the mid-1600s, the Standardbred is a product of American breeding some two-hundred years later.

In 1879, the National Association of Trotting Horse Breeders set forth a set of rules for Standardbreds being admitted into the American Trotter Register. To qualify, the horse had to trot a mile in two minutes, thirty seconds, and trace its lineage back to Justin Morgan, the stallion from which all registered Standardbreds descend.

Solomon looked forward to the exciting adventure of raising and breeding these fine horses with a great deal of enthusiasm.

Soon after the birth of their second child, a daughter named Anna Mae after her mother, Jacob Wickey asked Solomon to move back to Berne. Failing health prompted the request. He and Elizabeth needed help, he pleaded, due to the infirmities of old age.

Without doubt, we are bound to those we love always and forever. Amish family ties are strong; unbreakable. So, Solomon and Anna Mae and their two young children left their new home and comfortable surroundings in the Grabill community and moved to Berne, where they lived with Jacob and Elizabeth for a few months until they could find a place of their own. Before the birth of their third child, another daughter, Esther, they had moved not once, but twice.

In addition to doing field work and farm chores for his dad, Solomon also worked as crew foreman for his brother Amos's construction company, a job he would keep for nineteen years. He was happy with his life, with his work, and more often than not, he could be heard singing or yodeling as he set 2x4s or trim in place and drove nails.

In 1955, a FOR SALE sign was posted on forty acres of rich Adams County farmland with a two-story log house, a large barn, and several out-buildings located on county road 400-S in French Township. It was only a short distance west of the Wickey home place, and a stone's throw south of the farm owned by his sister, Emma, and her husband, Alvin Lambright. Solomon and Anna Mae bought the farm and moved into the house two weeks after the birth of their fourth child, Edith. Life was good! Very good!

The Log House on the 40 acres
(after new siding)

Wind Power Generator

The Community Phone Booth

Once they were settled and had time to catch their breath, Solomon was ready to concentrate on increasing his Standardbred herd. The few head of good registered breeding stock he acquired when he lived near Grabill were, of course, already contentedly grazing in his new Adams County pasture along county road 400-S.

During the next several years, in his quest for new bloodlines, Solomon attended both horse auctions and private sales in Indiana, Ohio, Pennsylvania, Kentucky, or anyplace registered Standardbreds were offered for sale. He was very selective, though, buying only the best.

Jacob Wickey was becoming much too feeble to care a whit about the farm or the livestock, so it was time to rid himself of the burden. He and Elizabeth sold the home place to Joseph and Rebecca Girod. Rebecca was comfortable living in the house Joseph built for her there, and it was important to her parents to make sure she would never have to move. Even though Jacob transferred ownership of the farm, he and Elizabeth lived there for the rest of their lives, in the same house where all of their children were born.

As part of the transfer, Jacob's livestock and farm equipment was sold to family and friends at private auction. Solomon was the successful high bidder on something that continues to be one of his most prized possessions....the little homemade wheelchair in which Rebecca rode like a princess when she was seven years old; the wheelchair filled with treasured childhood memories.

Solomon, now in a position to devote more time to raising horses, bought a young filly, the daughter of Leonard A. She was a beauty with slender, graceful lines and near perfect conformation. As a two-year-old he sold her to a gentleman engaged in harness racing, and she won twelve out of fourteen starts in her first year on the track.

He also owned several other exceptional colts sired by Leonard A., and eventually was the proud owner of Leonard A., a Standardbred stallion bred by Jack Robinson, owner of the well-known Wildwood Farm near Rome, Georgia. Leonard A. sired many colts of distinction which brought a steady stream of buyers to Solomon's door. None were sold at auction.

Solomon was almost as proud of his horses as he was of his children, but unlike his children, the horses couldn't tell him what hurt when they were sick, a situation he frequently prayed to God about. More often than not he acted as his own veterinarian, and always as his own farrier. He became an expert at corrective shoeing. He had a natural talent for balancing the shoe in order to balance the feet, thus enabling the horse to run clean.

One evening in the summer of 1976, Solomon's nephew, Dan I. Schwartz, and his wife, Lizzie, invited Solomon and Anna Mae to their home east of Berne to meet Frank Miesse, an herbalist and iridologist from Springfield, Ohio, who was going to introduce the science of iridology and explain the benefits of treating human ills with natural herbs. Solomon had absolutely no interest in the subject, and emphatically told Anna Mae that he was not going! But Anna Mae had already promised Lizzie they would be there, so they went.

Solomon sat near the front of the room where Frank Miesse stood beside a large, colorful iridology display chart detailing the iris of both the right and left eye, which, he said, was developed by Dr. Bernard Jensen after fifty-years of intense study and research.

He frequently pointed to the chart as he spoke, patiently explaining to those gathered that iridology is the kind of science that cannot be related through scientific tests, because it does not provide clinical information, but then, state-of-the-art tests in western medicine cannot reveal all of the answers either.

The subject was much more interesting than Solomon had anticipated, and he found himself paying rapt attention when someone in the back of the room asked, "Exactly what is iridology?" Frank answered by reading directly from Dr. Jensen's book:

Iridology is the science and practice that reveals inflammation, where it is located, and in what stage it is manifesting. The iris reveals body constitution, inherent weaknesses, levels of health and the transitions that take place in a person's body according to the way he lives.

Iridology is the science of analyzing the delicate structures of the iris of the eye. The iris is that portion of the eye that carries the color. Iris was the goddess of the rainbow in Greek Mythology; she was also messenger of the gods in the Iliad. Under magnification, the iris reveals itself to be a world of minute detail, a land of many features.

The iris represents a communication system capable of handling an amazing quantity of information.

The code reveals itself in the character of the individual iris fibers. There are uncounted numbers of these fibers present. The combination of various fiber characters make up an infinite variety.

Presently, as in the past, many primary health care doctors have used this form of analysis along with other diagnostic techniques to facilitate a more complete understanding of their patient's health care needs.

The eyes have been proclaimed throughout the ages as the window of the soul. We now acknowledge them as the mirror of the body. Manifestations in and about the eyes have long been used to gain insight into a person's state of health. Today it is realized that the information revealed in the eyes is greater than was formerly imagined.

A closer inspection with the tools made available by our expanding technology is revealing the iris to be a micro computer readout of bodily function and condition that truly merits every thinking man's honest and fair-minded consideration.

Through the application of iridology, it is possible to observe normal and abnormal reflex signs. It does not compare all people together to create a normal, but rather, compares an individual's strengths to their weaknesses; a weak organ in a strong body produces different characteristics, yet it is still a weakness for that person.*

"I think I understand what iridology is," the questioner stated, "but how does it work?"

Frank simply turned the page and continued reading:

The iris of the eye is the most complex tissue of the body meeting the outside world. It is an extension of the brain, being incredibly endowed with hundreds of thousands of nerve endings, microscopic blood vessels, muscle, and other tissues.

The iris is connected to every organ and tissue of the body by way of the brain and nervous system. The nerve fibers receive their impulses by way of the connections to the optic nerve, optic thalami, and spinal cord. They are formed embryologically from mesoderm and neuroectoderm tissues. Both sympathetic and parasympathic nervous systems are present in the iris.

In this way, Nature has provided us with a miniature television screen showing the most remote portions of the body by way of nerve reflex responses. We are discovering that the eye works two ways; not only does it enable us to bring images of the outside world within, it also shows images of what is within to the outside.*

Frank explained that by following the chart like a map, areas of weakness or inflammation can be located quickly. And once that is done, he told his students, the appropriate herbs and nutrition will lead the body back to optimal health.

By the time Frank Miesse had finished speaking, Solomon was brimming with excitement. His brain was spinning with questions; many more than time permitted asking that evening. Iridology. Yes, he felt sure that it, along with herbs, was the answer to his prayers about how his horses could tell him when they were ailing, and the herb chart would guide him to the proper treatment.

*Permission to reprint this text from his book, **Iridology Simplified,** was granted by the author, Dr. Bernard Jensen, Escondido, California, prior to his death.

At the conclusion of the meeting, he asked Frank if iridology and herbs would also benefit animals; horses in particular? It was a question Frank couldn't answer since he'd never considered the possibility before, but he promised Solomon he would find out and get back to him.

The evening had definitely been well spent, and at the end of the meeting when Frank announced that he and his sister-in-law, Rose Ann Miesse, would hold a series of weekly training classes in nearby Celina, Ohio, for anyone interested in learning more, the names of Solomon J. Wickey and Dan I. Schwartz, along with their wives, were at the top of the sign-up sheet.

Before they left the meeting that evening, Anna Mae picked up some literature about Nature's Sunshine Herbs to take home, while Solomon bought a copy of one of Dr. Jensen's books, which he intended to begin studying before sunrise the next morning.

In every life there is a moment, an event or a realization, that changes life irrevocably. Inevitably, in that precise moment, God sends some one, or some thing, to point the way. For Solomon, that moment was his introduction to the science of iridology, and even though the destination was uncertain, he welcomed his rendezvous with destiny without hesitation.

I know the plans I have for you, declared the Lord;
Plans to prosper you,
Plans not to harm you,
Plans to give you hope, and a future.

Jeremiah 29:11

FIVE

Solomon tossed and turned first one way, then another, as the sleepless night dragged by. His thoughts raced unbridled in a hundred different directions at once reviewing everything he had seen and heard at the meeting. Iridology. He knew it was the answer! Finally, he slipped out of bed, got dressed, quietly went downstairs, lighted a lamp, and began reading his new Dr. Jensen book.

Long before breakfast he was in the barn peering into first one horse's eyes, then another. They were all different, yet the same. He was intrigued; fascinated.

Throughout the coming week, every spare minute after work at the construction company was spent reading and studying Dr. Jensen's book, or gazing intently into a horse's large, revealing eyes to familiarize himself with their many similarities, and differences.

By the time he, Anna Mae, Dan and Lizzie arrived at the bank building in Celina the following week, his pocket bulged with a long list of questions, some of which were answered by Frank Miesse as the class proceeded, but there were many others he did not hesitate to ask. Much later Frank admitted that, at the time, he thought Solomon was as dumb as a coal bucket because he asked so many questions while, in fact, it was a sharp, curious, fertile mind he was dealing with. From Solomon's perspective, one answer only led to ten additional probing questions. He knew he wouldn't get answers if he didn't ask questions, and he was determined to have answers.

Solomon studied the iridology charts at every opportunity, memorized every tiny detail, and was absolutely amazed at the vast amount of information contained in the iris of the eye. To satisfy his insatiable search for more information on the subject, he read a variety of iridology books written by both Dr. Jensen and Dr. Joseph Deck, a German author, and armed with a new magnified iridology glass, he practiced on Anna Mae, their children, Dan, Lizzie, co-workers, anybody, everybody.

Solomon eagerly anticipated the weekly trips to Celina. Each class provided a new learning experience, another opportunity to find answers to the many questions raised through his study and practice the previous week.

Frank Miesse was, first and foremost, a Baptist minister who had been blessed with a keen intuitive ability. According to Solomon, he was also an excellent teacher; one with an extensive knowledge of herbs and herbal nutrition. He had a passion for investigating both the historical use, and the value of all herbs, a passion quickly embraced by Solomon, the gardener. Frank selected a different group of herbs every week, which he went over in detail with the class, patiently explaining the use and benefit of each herb listed on the comprehensive historical herb chart that he handed out as part of the lesson material.

When the series of weekly training classes ended, Solomon was not only excited about the benefits of iridology, he was also quite adept at locating and isolating weaknesses in the body. He seemed to have a natural talent for choosing the herb that would best correct that weakness. Solomon was thrilled when co-workers who pooh-poohed him and iridology in the beginning, quickly changed their tunes as their own health began to improve significantly.

While they were still going to class, Anna Mae took charge of buying the herbs. She ordered a good supply of the Nature's Sunshine products that Frank recommended, along with herbs to fill orders coming in from family and friends, and, of course, herbs for Solomon's horses. Solomon refused to accept payment for his services, but did agree to sell herbs to people who had a need. Even though neither Solomon nor Anna Mae realized it at the time, their lives had suddenly changed direction.

Sick people, perfect strangers, began knocking on Solomon's door asking for help, and refused to leave when they were told he was at work. Instead, they insisted on waiting until he returned, regardless of the hour. Not only did he miss meals, he also lost sleep. When he looked tired the next day, instead of sympathizing, his non-Amish co-workers (the English) admitted that they told their ailing friends and relatives about him, about iridology, and about the positive results they, themselves, had had. They also told them where Solomon lived, and suggested they go see him.

As word spread, growing numbers of sick people appeared at Solomon's door, even though in typical Amish tradition his name was not on his mailbox, nor was there any other visible sign to indicate he lived there. Nonetheless, before he got out of bed every morning vehicles bearing license plates from all over Indiana and surrounding states were lined up in his driveway, and, more often than not, down the county road who knows how far.

Day after day Solomon agonized over the deplorable condition of those barely-alive bodies being dragged through his door. He routinely heard sad stories of previously diagnosed incurable disease, lengthy chronic illnesses, unsuccessful surgeries, injuries, and more. Some shuffled along dragging oxygen tanks. Some were little more than overly medicated zombies. Many felt helpless, hopeless, after being told they had only a few months, or weeks, to live, and frequently tears trickled uncontrollably down their cheeks as they spoke of a grim, bleak future or no future at all. Solomon, they said, was their last desperate hope.

Although he made it clear that he was not a doctor, he listened compassionately but routinely ignored their reports of doom and gloom. Instead, he picked up an iridology glass and went to work. Invariably, their eyes told a very different story. After carefully checking the iris, he would lean back in his swivel chair, pause a moment, then very confidently explain the inherent weaknesses the eyes showed manifesting in the body, and how those conditions could be reversed through the use of herbs. Some people just stared at him, simultaneously stunned and relieved. Lives changed. Sagging postures straightened, face and jaw muscles relaxed, eyes brightened with new hope. Misery and despair gave way to joy; optimism; euphoria. Those special moments were Solomon's greatest reward.

If they had questions he answered them in simple terms they could understand. Sometimes he handed the iridology glass to the person's mate as he pointed out the affected area, and explained how the iris of the eye would change as the body returned to normal. Solomon never hurried. Regardless of the number of people filling the waiting room, he took time to talk to the person sitting in front of him; to reassure them, to give them hope.

People came without an appointment and patiently waited their turn. Whether or not they returned was their own decision. He did not tell them to come back, nor did he keep records of any kind. He didn't even ask their name. It was not necessary.

Solomon was forced to quit his job at the construction company because of the steady stream of people lined up in his front yard. Normally, he saw the first person about six o'clock in the morning, and many times the last one didn't leave before two o'clock the next morning. This went on six days a week, every week, without end.

At first he invited people into his house, but as their numbers steadily increased that practice became unfair to his family. Out of necessity, he built a sixty-foot by eighty-foot metal building... actually it was an extension to the buggy shed on the north side of the barn...which he referred to as *the shop.*

It was a simple, functional, rectangular building with a front door, a back door, and several windows. Inside, he built sturdy floor to ceiling wood shelves along the front side of a partition wall to accommodate hundreds of bottles of herbs, then just a step away, added a long sales counter facing the large waiting room. Solomon's work area, located down a short hallway behind the partition wall, was furnished with four or five straight, solid oak chairs and a small walnut desk tucked below a stack of shallow shelves that held dozens of bottles containing a variety of herbs. Another shelf accommodated an assortment of iridology and other health related reference books. The building was heated by a coal stove, cooled by natural breezes blowing through open windows, and was lighted by kerosene lamps. A well-used path led to an outhouse.

Solomon's shop was a sharp contrast to plush offices in the city with comfortable chairs, crisp sheets, polished stainless steel instruments, case histories, records, and forms to fill out. Solomon had no help, other than Anna Mae and their older children who took turns working behind the sales counter. To many, Solomon's shop was a heavenly oasis surrounded by the peaceful, unhurried serenity of Amish farm life, a place oozing with contentment, good health, and above all, hope.

41

Solomon's first Herb Shop & Office

To people filled with disease and despair, the experience of the place was, in itself, uplifting; comforting; tranquilizing.

On a normal day, Solomon saw as many as one-hundred people, but his success and growing reputation did not set well with one of his brothers. Perhaps it was envy, or jealous resentment, or just the continuation of an intense childhood sibling rivalry. Brother had always complained that it wasn't fair for Solomon to have all the good luck. Solomon was smarter, he said. He could draw perfect pictures...of horses, and such...and sing, and yodel, and then, of course, he didn't have just any old horses like everybody else, he had registered Standardbreds. And now the greatest insult of all; he was becoming famous. It was simply too much to bear!

The ringleaders, Solomon's jealous brother and his best buddy, along with a small handful of Old Order Amish men from the church district who were easily influenced, questioned the goings-on day after day, night after night, at Solomon's place, and they did not hesitate to sneak around outside the shop under cover of darkness playing detective. Solomon was keenly aware of their presence, and recognized the inquisitive eyes shaded by black, broad brimmed hats peering at him through windows shadowed by flickering lamp light.

Brother and his buddy, both highly suspicious individuals by nature, were absolutely incensed by the notion that Solomon was consorting with the Devil...and they steadfastly refused to believe there was any truth, whatsoever, to rumors circulating around Berne that Solomon had been blessed by a special gift from God. If God was passing out gifts, they theorized indignantly between tobacco splats to the ground, why weren't the two of them included?

No, they prophesied, gazing into someone's eye for a few seconds through a small, strange looking glass, and telling them that swallowing a few herbs would restore their health, definitely had to be the work of the Devil. Witchcraft! Yes, indeed, they agreed, Solomon would bear watching. Neither of them found it necessary, however, to question the activities of Dan I. Schwartz who was equally as busy with an on-going day to day iridology and herb business as was Solomon.

The next few years were unusually busy for the Wickeys. Solomon and Anna Mae, along with Dan and Lizzie Schwartz, continued making the trip to Celina once a month for an evening with Frank Miesse, or occasionally, a guest speaker. Solomon read everything on the subject of iridology, herbs and nutrition he could get his hands on, but his greatest teachers, by far, were the people he saw every day. They challenged him to ask questions; to seek answers.

In the coming months Solomon attended a number of iridology classes, lectures and seminars, including an excellent, informative class held in Columbus, Ohio, and taught by Jack Richardson, a well known herbalist from Nature's Sunshine's home office in Utah.

Solomon even taught a few classes, himself. He rented the community room in a bank building in Bluffton, Indiana, and enrolled small groups of not more than ten students for each series of weekly training classes. It was an exciting new experience; also quite rewarding when each class produced at least one or two outstanding new iridologists.

The Troublemakers, however, were not favorably impressed by Solomon's latest achievement, so they took their spiteful, malicious accusations to the Preacher in their church district for solace. He, in turn, made an official call on Solomon, taking him to task, demanding to know exactly what he was doing, and how much money he was making from the effort. Obviously money was his primary concern.

Solomon explained that herbs were available at his shop for people who wanted to buy them. He said that after reading the iris of a person's eyes, he usually made a list of the herbs known to correct the weaknesses he had found, and handed it to them, but where, or even if, they bought any of those herbs was strictly their own decision. He and Anna Mae sold herbs at their own wholesale cost, he said, not at retail. Solomon made it clear that their only income from the business was a monthly commission check from Nature's Sunshine based on the volume of products ordered. Nor, he emphatically emphasized, did he accept payment for iridology consultations. The company's monthly commission check. That was it!

In his most stern tone of voice, while pointing a long index finger at Solomon, the Preacher cautioned that making money other than by the sweat of one's brow was unholy, against Amish law, and would have to stop. Solomon steadfastly held his ground. He stated that from the beginning it was his intention to use iridology and herbs to treat his horses, but apparently it was God's intention that his priority should be helping human beings instead.

He insisted that his strong faith, along with the knowledge of plants he gained through gardening, the knowledge of anatomy he acquired through butchering, his compassion for people suffering prolonged illnesses and afflictions, indeed, every experience, everything he'd done since childhood, had prepared him for this, his destined life's work.

The wind went out of the Preacher's sails when Solomon reminded him of the large number of Old Order Amish from various other church districts in Indiana and surrounding states who regularly brought their health problems to him.

Solomon invited him to check with his dad if he had questions about Old Order Amish law regarding his work. Jacob Wickey whiled away many hours with his son at the shop. He loved sitting-in, observing, and talking to the people. Unlike the Troublemakers, he knew first hand what Solomon was doing, as well as how grateful people were for the life-changing service.

Even though the frailty of old age had slowed him down physically, Jacob Wickey was just as mentally sharp as ever, and would be an Old Order Amish minister with a reputation for strict adherence to the Scriptures for as long as he lived. If Solomon's work violated the Scriptures in any way, whatsoever, he would've been the first to bring it to his attention and order him to stop.

The Preacher left in a huff. Solomon continued business as usual…at least for the time being.

Solomon held a series of evening lectures in his shop to meet the increasing demand for information about herbs, their uses and benefits. An excellent teacher with a growing reputation for being an exceptionally knowledgeable herbalist, he consistently drew crowds of about eighty people from Indiana, Ohio, Pennsylvania, and surrounding states.

Occasionally someone would come to him after a lecture, asking if they could sit-in with him at the shop for on-the-spot training by observation. More often than not he obligingly agreed.

Wendell Whitman was one of those people who studied with Solomon in this manner every week for four years before he founded the very successful Trinity College of Natural Health in Warsaw, Indiana. Wendell asked Solomon to be a partner in the new enterprise, but he declined the offer.

The Troublemaking peeping toms, who were even busier than usual trying to keep up with these new goings-on at Solomon's shop, encouraged the Preacher to make another official call on Solomon, which he did. He ordered Solomon to cut back to five days a week. Working in the shop on Saturday would no longer be tolerated, he said. Solomon knew it was coming, so quietly agreed to comply. It was an order which, according to the Preacher, was not debatable.

Even though work consumed most of their time, Solomon and Anna Mae managed to have a normal Amish social life. They rarely, if ever, missed church, and regularly participated in church activities with their many loyal, supportive friends, relatives and neighbors.

His family continued to be of the utmost importance to Solomon. He loved, cherished, and appreciated his wife and each precious child. In the fourteen years since moving into the log house west of Berne, he and Anna Mae had been blessed by the birth of six healthy sons; Jerry, Solomon Jr., Marvin, Alvin, Jacob and Levi.

Once in a while Solomon set work aside and arranged for family outings, including an occasional trip to his favorite horse auction held in Delaware, Ohio, where bidding among Amish buyers was fierce. These trips excited the older boys, particularly David, Jerry and Solomon Jr. For these up-and-coming young horsemen, each trip provided an opportunity to learn, to have a picnic, and to enjoy the company of other Amish boys their own age. Anna Mae and the girls appreciated the day away from home, too. Anna Mae visited with the women, while the girls glanced at boys, blushed, and giggled with their teenage girlfriends.

1979 was a year filled with both happiness and sadness for the Wickeys. Solomon and Anna Mae were honored when Nature's Sunshine presented them with a beautiful plaque for outstanding achievement. Anna Mae gave birth to a son, Joseph, another joyous occasion, but in November, Solomon's spirit was saddened by the death of his dad. His beloved mother died exactly one year later, in November, 1980.

One day Charles H. Barber, an old gentleman from Ft. Wayne, came to the shop to see Solomon. He had owned and operated a local stone quarry for many years, but like so many others, it was not until after he retired that he had time to devote to things which really piqued his interest.

Charles' good friend, Dr. Bernard Jensen, told him about Solomon, and about the fine work he was doing with iridology, and with herbs. He decided it was worth a trip to Adams County to meet this man whom Dr. Jensen held in such high regard.

Charles and Solomon became friends. Charles spent a considerable amount of time at the shop where the two men compared notes and tossed ideas back and forth. For some length of time Charles had been interested in communicating with the body through muscle testing, and he shared his knowledge of the skill with Solomon. It was the significant breakthrough Solomon had been looking for. He immediately began using the technique, a method he found to be fast, precise, and reliable in pinpointing specific problems.

*****

Throughout the night a strong, unrelenting wind had piled falling snow into high drifts, burying fences alongside flat roadways from one end of Adams County to the other. Even though a county highway snowplow had partially cleared road 400-S past the Wickey place shortly before dawn, Solomon was surprised to see a bright red 4-wheel-drive pickup truck crunch its way into his driveway.

48

By the time he and his four older sons pulled on heavy jackets and slapped black broad brimmed hats onto their heads as they rushed out the back door, Solomon's good friend, Bob Black, had lowered the tailgate, exposing two shiny new snowmobiles.

"You think you can drive one of these?" Bob yelled to Solomon as he made his way through the deep white stuff.

"I'm absolutely sure I can!" Solomon yelled back confidently, "but I would be shunned forever if I got caught."

He helped Bob lift one of the snowmobiles out of the truck, and watched as he demonstrated its capabilities by cutting didos every which way across the snow. Solomon, in his late thirties at the time, as was Bob, was like a daredevil itching for a new adventure. No question about it, he was determined to ride that machine, and reasoned that even though he was not allowed to drive it, it would not violate Amish rules if he was merely a passenger riding on the seat behind Bob. So away they went down the road, across an open field, twisting and turning, leaving snow spewing behind them like thousands of tiny effervescent geysers amidst Solomon's gleeful squeals.

Once back in the driveway, Solomon walked around the snowmobile, stroking his beard, observing its every detail.

"How fast did we go?" he asked.

"About 60," Bob replied.

"Is that as fast as it will go?" Solomon shot back.

"No," Bob shook his head. "It'll do about 95."

"Well, let's try it out!" Solomon challenged, excitedly jumping around in the snow, eager for another ride.

"OK. Let's go!" Bob yelled.

While Solomon went to the house to exchange his traditional hat for a close-fitting stocking cap, Bob took a few minutes to plan the race. In order to keep the glint of the bright morning sun behind them, they would travel from east to west on the smooth, cleared surface of road 400-S. And, on second thought, he sent the four boys to stand guard at the nearby crossroad intersection to stop any possible oncoming traffic.

When everything was ready, Bob and Solomon climbed aboard and headed east on road 400-S in search of a suitable starting point. Once there, Bob whipped the snowmobile around, stopped momentarily to rev the engine, then opened the throttle, and away they flew. The speedometer registered 92 as they whizzed past the boys guarding the intersection.

Wow! What a thrill for Solomon, a man who loves speed; fast horses, boats, cars, trains, and airplanes, although he had never flown in one. The experience, the exhilaration of flying together across fresh, unsullied snow on that cold winter morning would forever remain in the memory of each of these fun-loving men who were destined to become good friends.

Bob and his wife, Jan, lived in Ft. Wayne where he worked at the International Harvester plant. In 1979, Jan became very ill and went through an exhausting series of diagnostic tests ordered by several medical doctors, all of whom had a different opinion about her health crisis, but those tests shed little, if any, light on the cause of her problem.

Out of frustration and desperation, Bob made an appointment for her to see a doctor at the Mayo Clinic in Rochester, Minnesota. However, in the meantime, one of his friends from Harvester told him that if he wanted to know what was wrong with his wife, Solomon Wickey would have the answer in about five minutes without a single painful test. Being the curious person that he was, the very next evening Bob and Jan drove down to Solomon's place, arriving about seven o'clock. They were quite surprised to find more than thirty people ahead of them patiently waiting their turn.

Bob and Jan finally walked into Solomon's office about midnight. As the men shook hands, Jan sat down in a straight chair directly in front of Solomon. He looked into her eyes for a few seconds through his iridology glass, and immediately said, "I don't know what kind of nervous stress you're under, but whatever it is you have to make some changes **right now!**

Bob wondered what was wrong with this kook, because their medical specialist had specifically said that, even though he didn't know exactly what was causing Jan's illness, he was absolutely sure it was not nerve or stress related.

Solomon studied her eyes for another few seconds through the glass, then explained that her eyes told him her extreme nerve stress was having an effect on the gallbladder, causing it to put out a poisonous toxin, throwing the pancreas and spleen off. He suggested a couple of herbs that would help the situation, wrote them down, and handed the paper to Jan.

In less than ten minutes after they walked into his office, they walked out. Neither of them knew anything about using herbs to heal the body, so they left without making a purchase.

Bob and Jan kept their scheduled appointment at the Mayo Clinic, arriving there late the following Tuesday evening. Over the next day-and-a-half Jan underwent a series of twenty-six exhausting tests. When she and Bob went for their diagnostic consultation on Thursday afternoon, the doctor said the extreme nerve stress was having an effect on the gallbladder, pancreas and spleen. It sounded like an echo, because they heard the very same words in the very same sequence from Solomon Wickey just a few days before. There really must be something to iridology after all!

They stayed in Rochester for five weeks while Jan underwent therapy to teach her how to say "No," and how to recognize her stress limits and deal with them.

As soon as they returned home the first week in September, they immediately went to Berne to see Solomon. When he looked in Jan's eyes, he blurted out, "Where did all of these drug spots come from?"

Bob told him about the trip to the Mayo Clinic, about all of the tests, and about the identical findings. Solomon was not surprised in the least, but he said it would be several weeks before the dyes and chemicals from all those tests were flushed out of Jan's body.

Mostly out of curiosity, Bob took his turn sitting in the chair in front of Solomon that day, and was shocked when Solomon asked how long he had been asthmatic.

"How in the world do you know I'm asthmatic?" Bob asked.

"Because," Solomon explained, "your eyes are showing me a huge amount of mucus congestion around your entire body."

Bob readily admitted that he had suffered from asthma for the past eighteen years, and was very encouraged when Solomon leaned back in his swivel chair and quietly said, "You don't have to go through life like that."

Eleven months later, using the herbs and diet Solomon recommended, Bob was totally free of both asthma and hay fever, as well as a long list of allergies that had plagued him since childhood.

Early the next spring when Bob received an invitation to attend an iridology class Solomon would be teaching in Bluffton, Indiana, he went. He was highly impressed by Solomon's vast knowledge of iridology and how the human body works, and he took a couple of books on the subject home with him, but his busy work schedule did not permit time to delve into a serious, concentrated study of iridology at that particular time. However, when union workers at International Harvester walked out on strike later that year, he had plenty of time to study.

With Solomon's encouragement, Bob became a distributor of Nature's Sunshine products in November, 1979, and for the next six months, he spent four days a week in the office with Solomon, studying, observing, and learning everything he could about iridology, the human body, herbs, and optimal health. He opened his own office in Ft. Wayne in the summer of 1980.

When Bob learned that Dr. Bernard Jensen would be teaching a three-day iridology seminar that fall at TAN-TAR-A Resort, located at Osage Beach on the eastern edge of the Lake of the Ozarks in south central Missouri, he thought he and Solomon should attend. Solomon, who greatly admired Dr. Jensen, and just happened to love traveling, quickly agreed. Away they went to beautiful TAN-TAR-A in Bob's Cadillac; ladies sitting in back, gents up front.

TAN-TAR-A Resort Hotel and Villa Suites was everything they expected, and more. Bob and Solomon rented adjoining villa suites not fifty feet from water's edge where they could sit on the patio sipping coffee and watch fish jump while colorful sail boats drifted lazily in the distance. They even caught a fish or two.

Solomon and Bob enjoyed Dr. Jensen, and would long remember the brotherhood, as well as new information the Master of Iridology so generously shared with them. While Dr. Jensen occupied the men, Jan and Anna Mae relaxed, talked, laughed, and browsed through every nook and cranny they could find. When they ran out of steam, they refreshed themselves with tall glasses of iced tea and generous slices of fresh strawberry pie. As a result, they were affectionately dubbed, *the Strawberry Twins.*

One evening when the four of them were out for a leisurely stroll around the grounds, Bob accidentally stepped on the hem of

Anna Mae's skirt. She whipped around to face him and gruffly snapped, "You stepped on my dress! Get off my dress!"

Bob stopped dead in his tracks, too embarrassed and humiliated to speak. Later, Solomon swore he'd never before seen color drain from a man's face so fast. Anna Mae was only teasing, of course, but Bob thought she was serious until Solomon broke into gales of laughter. From then on, Bob and Anna Mae stayed awake nights trying to think of tricks to play on each other.

Back at home, a young college student found her way to Solomon's shop. She explained that she had chosen iridology as her topic for a class assignment, and wanted to enroll in Solomon's next class. He was delighted.

She proved to be an unusually bright, inquisitive student; one who kept him on his toes. She reminded him of his own enthusiasm, his constant questions, when he traveled that same path. Like Solomon, she soaked up information like a sponge, diligently studied the iridology and herb charts, and instinctively knew what to do in every situation.

In addition to being a frequent visitor to Solomon's shop to observe how he dealt with the diverse ailments people brought to him every day, she worked part time for a local veterinarian specializing in equine medicine, and as one might expect, Solomon told her it was his original intention to study iridology for the sole purpose of treating his own horses.

He welcomed having her around, and it wasn't long before she was spending a considerable amount of time in his barnyard with the Standardbreds. In response to her many inquiries and theories, Solomon ended up developing an iridology chart for horses; the first such chart ever created for animals.

With a copy of the new chart in hand, she introduced iridology to her boss as a dependable, accurate diagnostic tool, and went one step further by recommending herbs as a reliable, less invasive method of treatment. The doctor was most impressed by the iridology chart, and found her research fascinating, as did her college professor and classmates. At the end of the semester she won an award for outstanding achievement, along with a tidy sum of cash.

During the next several years, as word about his iridology chart for horses spread, Solomon taught a number of classes for veterinarians engaged in equine practice.

The herb business was growing by leaps and bounds as a result of sales to new customers and re-orders from established customers. Even though they were doing well financially, Solomon and Anna Mae continued to be very conservative. Solomon paid off the mortgage on the farm, and had money in the bank.

It galled the Troublemakers to watch a United Parcel truck turn into Solomon's driveway five days every week to deliver large boxes of product and pick up orders being sent out. All they could think about, or talk about, was the money they thought he was making. Greed, envy, and even hatred, nearly drove them insane when they learned that Solomon had paid off the mortgage on his farm, while they, themselves, were struggling to meet note payments. It just wasn't fair!

Now that Jacob Wickey was not there to stick up for Solomon, the Troublemakers once again sniveled and whined to the sympathetic Preacher, who was behind in the mortgage payments on his own farm. He made another official call to inform Solomon that he would no longer be working in his shop on Friday, but he came up short when Solomon challenged him, demanding to know upon which Biblical Scripture, chapter and verse, he based that order. (In the Old Order Amish faith, all accusations must be backed up by Scripture).

The Preacher's attempt to answer was pathetically feeble, but for the sake of peace and harmony in the church district, Solomon closed his shop on Friday, wondering how long it would be before the Preacher tried to chop off another day...or force him to close forever.

But at the moment, the new schedule was actually welcome. It gave Solomon time to do other things. For example, he had something new, exciting and entertaining to occupy his attention. Namely, twin sons, Ervin and Mervin, born October 6, 1981. These twin sons completed their family of thirteen children; three girls, ten boys.

Solomon refused to allow the Preacher's latest proclamation to slow him down. In addition to helping Anna Mae with the twins, he worked long hours, since there was no shortage of sick people finding their way to his shop. Experience had taught him to work much more efficiently, so by the end of a four day work week, he had seen approximately the same number of people as before, give or take a few.

The Troublemakers were livid! The new schedule did not produce the results they had expected, but then, nothing short of a huge padlock on the door to Solomon's shop would satisfy them. In their judgment, he was still making too much money, whatever the amount.

The twins were about eighteen months old when the Preacher made his next official visit on behalf of himself and the envious Troublemakers, to inform Solomon that his shop would be closed permanently.

Once again Solomon fought back. He refused to comply with the new order without proof that he was going against Amish law as set forth in the Scriptures. He asked the Preacher to quote the Tenth Commandment, and when he refused, Solomon recited it:

> "Thou shalt not covet thy neighbour's house, thou shalt not covet thy neighbour's wife, nor his manservant, nor his maidservant, nor his ox, nor his ass, nor anything that is thy neighbour's."

The Preacher hated Solomon for making him look like the covetous hypocrite he was, but after a sizzling, humiliating Swiss-German verbal exchange, he agreed to allow Solomon to work in the shop three days a week; Monday, Tuesday, and Wednesday. And, he promised there would be no further official visits to change that schedule.

Two very active little boys occupied most of Anna Mae's time. The girls, Anna Mae Jr., Esther, and Edith, were all young ladies, much too busy to spend time behind the sales counter in the shop everyday, so some of the older boys took turns working there, albeit begrudgingly.

Solomon decided it was time to make some changes. He posted a sign on the front door of his shop announcing his new hours:

Monday – Walk in

Tuesday and Wednesday – by Appointment Only

**"If you need a good doctor,
get a veterinarian.
Animals can't tell him what's wrong,
he's just got to know."**

Will Rogers

SIX

The events of 1983 would change Solomon Wickey's life forever!

Solomon met Dr. Eugene Watkins in 1976, soon after he became interested in herbs and iridology. They met when Dr. Watkins, one of the foremost authorities on herbs in the United States, presented a lecture at Frank Miesse's place in Ohio, which Solomon and Anna Mae and Dan and Lizzie Schwartz attended.

Dr. Eugene Watkins was impressed by Solomon because he was like a sponge seeking answers to many thought-provoking questions; a man who was sincerely eager to learn everything he could about herbs and their uses. That first meeting was the beginning of what would become a longstanding mutual respect and friendship between the two men.

Herbs as a business was still in its infancy in the 1970s, but as Dr. Watkins traveled throughout the United States and Canada teaching and lecturing on the subject, it became increasingly clear to him that there was a growing need for herbs in liquid form that would provide immediate relief by getting into the blood stream much faster than the conventional capsules or powders.

With the assistance of his wife, Dr. Watkins began mixing and bottling his own pure herbal extracts at home. As soon as the public discovered these wonderful new liquid herbs, he had to hire two helpers, but even so, he simply could not meet the overwhelming demand for his products.

Early in 1983, Dr. Watkins turned his cottage industry into a bona fide business venture. He chose Andrew David Harrison to be his partner, and together, they found the perfect building in a Detroit suburb that would accommodate administrative offices, a manufacturing plant, and space for a much needed warehouse and shipping dock. The next important challenge for the new company was national distribution of its products.

Dr. Watkins made a trip to Berne to see his friend, Solomon Wickey, whose huge success in selling and distributing Nature's Sunshine products was widely known, and envied, by many of those in the herbal products industry.

Dr. Watkins said, "Solomon, we're going to start a company now, since we're able to make enough product for wide distribution. We want to put this on a solid business basis, and we need your help."

Since Solomon had been privileged to preview some of Dr. Watkins' liquid herbal formulas, he was already impressed by their benefits and exceptional quality. He knew, without a doubt, that Dr. Watkins and Andrew David Harrison manufactured the very finest liquid herbal products available in the USA, and was highly honored when his friend asked him to be the new company's first distributor.

Solomon smiled and nodded agreement. And so it was, that with a simple binding handshake, Solomon J. Wickey became **Distributor # 1 for PURE HERBS, LTD.** Quite an accomplishment for a man only working three days a week from a small building in his barnyard, without electricity, a telephone, or an automobile.

*****

Bob Black was both pleased and excited when Solomon suggested they teach a class together in the spring of 1983, and he quickly agreed.

When Bob arrived at the community room located in the basement of a bank building in Bluffton, Indiana where the class was being held, Solomon greeted him with the news that he would have to teach the class by himself. Bob had attended many iridology and herb classes, but teach one? Him? He froze at the very thought.

"No way, Buddy!" he exclaimed apprehensively.

"You don't have a choice," Solomon replied. "Late this afternoon the Preacher stopped by my place to inform me that I will no longer be permitted to stand up in front of English people to talk about herbs, or iridology, or anything else for that matter. I'll be sitting right there on the front row to answer questions, but you're gonna have to be the main speaker."

Bob felt like the pegs had been knocked out from under him. He stood there with a blank stare on his face unable to speak, even though his brain was screaming, "No! No!" He just didn't have the self confidence to teach a class. However, the anguish on Solomon's face clearly told him this was not a joke, so he walked outside to his truck, took three capsules of a calming herb to settle his nerves and quiet the butterflies in his stomach, and had a quick talk with the Lord. He went back into the classroom and confidently walked to the podium to welcome the new students.

Once he relaxed words seemed to tumble out of his mouth and before he knew it, it was time to open for questions, which, naturally, he directed to Solomon. The entire program went very smoothly. The audience never suspected that Bob and Solomon were not following a well-planned format. Bob had a ball. He was hooked. This was only the first of many such classes taught by the Wickey-Black team.

The Preacher was furious. After all, he reasoned, he was the Völliger Diener, the spiritual leader of the congregation. As such, one of his duties was to control every Old Order Amish person living in his church district, but he was at his wits end with Solomon Wickey's defiant attitude.

When he ordered Solomon to stop speaking in front of English people, he thought he had made it crystal clear that there would be no more classes for the public. Not ever. But, as usual, Solomon found a way around the order. His arrogant disobedience was exasperating. In the Preacher's way of thinking, Solomon did not show the proper respect for him, or for his position in the church, or for his absolute authority.

At least one of the Preacher's deductions was correct. At that particular time, several men in the church district, including Solomon, questioned not only the Preacher's authority, but also his continued leadership.

The Preacher's moral compass had broken. Actually, it had been irreparably shattered. Rumors about his conduct and moral transgressions spread like wild fire throughout his church district, as well as through the various other neighboring Amish church districts and the Berne community. He was fifty-one years old, and even though he had a good wife and nine children, the youngest fifteen years old, he was accused of breaking the Ten Commandments by stepping outside his faith to have a steamy, illicit affair with a young local English woman.

Among those in the church district there was talk of little else, but when in earshot of outsiders, they maintained their silence. Not so with the townspeople. They were anything but silent. English tongues wagged even more briskly than usual as they watched the truth of the rumors grow larger by the month.

Amish women curtailed, or even cancelled, shopping trips into town to avoid the embarrassment of questions and snickers. For some of the Amish men the Preacher became an instant hero. Others favored petitioning the council of Old Order Amish Bishops to transfer him out of their district, or to expel him from the order altogether. The Preacher was a hypocrite, they said, hardly the kind of spiritual leader they wanted their children to look up to.

Solomon had always been a peaceful, gentle soul, hardly given to criticism or judgment of his fellow man. He kept his opinion of the Preacher, and his recent reckless adventure, to himself. But when he was called upon to express his thoughts on the subject, he did not hesitate to state his strong Christian views to those present. He pointed out, among other things, that he considered marriage vows to be sacred, and could not condone, or ignore, infidelity, adultery, or any other conduct unbecoming an Amish man of God. Therefore, if it came to a vote, he would stand with those asking for a replacement.

Sides were drawn. A tiny handful of the more devout followers of God's word lined up together. Several, mostly the younger men, supported the Preacher regardless of his transgressions. Others chose to remain neutral. The controversy raged for months without resolve.

As one might expect, the fact that Solomon had spoken out against keeping a leader engaged in this kind of behavior was quickly brought to the Preacher's attention by his loyal supporters.

Daytime temperatures soared into the high 90s, while rain gauges in Adams County remained bone dry. The unusually hot, dry weather only intensified the Preacher's anger. In his warped thinking, he was incensed with the idea that, for one reason or another, Solomon, and Solomon alone, was responsible for his problems. He couldn't stand to watch Solomon's continued prosperity week after week, while he struggled to plant corn and soybeans between dry, hard clods, hoping for rain; rain that refused to fall.

As sizzling, unrelenting heat bore down day after day, week after week, leaves on stunted corn stalks rolled into tight, flute-like cylinders and died from lack of moisture. Soybeans fared no better.

Horses and livestock stood aimlessly under trees in scorched pastures switching their tails, wishing for a blade of green grass to nibble. One of the strongest, and longest, drought and heat waves on record had a stranglehold on area farmers. Crop and pasture damage in Adams County was expected to top $7 million. Tempers were understandably short.

The combination of personal problems, heat, anger, and rage sent the Preacher over the edge. He made a trip to Decatur to demand county officials close Solomon's shop permanently. They refused, saying they knew of no legal grounds to do so. He left more determined than ever to find a way to bring Solomon Wickey to his knees; to put him out of business.

According to an eyewitness, his next stop was the health department in the neighboring Wells County seat in Bluffton where his complaints and accusations fell on a more sympathetic ear.

The Preacher's visit was just the stroke of good luck George Merkle had been praying for. Merkle, a medical doctor who was engaged in private family practice, also happened to be President of the Wells County Board of Health.

In recent years his own annual net income had taken a nose dive as increasing numbers of his patients found their way to Solomon's shop. In addition to his own loss of income, he also deeply resented the thousands of dollars being diverted away from other local medical doctors and hospitals because of Solomon and his herbs. On several occasions Dr. Merkle had tried to find a way to eliminate the competition.

For example, his recollection of two such incidents came to mind:

The Wells County Board of Health supposedly had a complaint from a citizen who said her grandson was taking a huge quantity of some kind of pills. Perhaps they were herbs and vitamins, she said. She really didn't know what they were.

It seems the four-year-old child's mother had taken him to see Solomon Wickey. After Solomon pinpointed the child's health problem, the mother purchased the herbs he suggested and was giving them to her son. Dr. Merkle heard the story from a nurse at Caylor-Nickel Clinic in Bluffton, who said the grandmother mentioned it to her in a casual conversation. Nothing factual; just hearsay.

Dr. Merkle brought the matter up for discussion at the next meeting of the board of health, and David G. Pietz, M.D., Chief County Health Officer, assigned his agent, Dennis Zawodni, the new Wells County Sanitarian, the task of investigating the complaint. It was Zawodni's first job. He was young, fresh out of college, and eager to please.

As county sanitarian, it was his job to inspect sewage, and sewage related problems, such as trash, garbage, and restaurant kitchens...hardly the criterion necessary to investigate someone whom Dr. Merkle wanted to accuse of practicing medicine without a license.

Zawodni was much too inexperienced to handle such an investigation. He was shrewd enough to know, however, that he had no jurisdiction to investigate anything going on in Adams County, so upon the advice of Dr. Merkle, he called Bob Murray in the drug control section of the Indiana State Board of Health, and asked him to conduct the investigation.

Some time later, when Bob Murray got around to complying with the request, he asked Dennis Zawodni to accompany him on an undercover visit to Solomon's herb shop, which he did.

After waiting their turn, the two gentlemen went into Solomon's office where Bob Murray acted as "the patient." As usual, Solomon looked in his eyes through the iridology lens, and found a problem Murray didn't know he had. Zawodni dutifully wrote down the name of an herb Solomon suggested.

Bob Murray offered payment, but Solomon refused, saying there was no charge. On his way out Murray stopped at the sales counter, bought the herb, and they left.

When he got back to Indianapolis he had it analyzed. The Indiana State Chemistry Laboratory verified that the contents were exactly as stated on the label.

Even though Murray's report did not contain a shred of concrete evidence to prove Solomon was doing anything wrong, Dr. Merkle ran to the Adams County prosecutor with a copy in hand, demanding he charge Solomon Wickey with practicing medicine without a license. Nothing came of it though, because the prosecutor refused to take legal action on the flimsy, frivolous complaint, which, in his judgment, was entirely without merit.

Solomon Wickey had saved the lives of several folks near and dear to the prosecutor, and continued to improve the quality of life for a growing number of his friends and co-workers. He gave Dr. Merkle the courtesy of briefly listening to his complaints and false accusations, but as he showed him the door, he warned the good doctor not to come back until he could display a dead body, along with absolute proof that Solomon Wickey had killed it.

Then there was another time Dr. Merkle remembered, when in 1980 he, himself, had gone to see Solomon, using an assumed name, of course, with a well-rehearsed cock-and-bull story. To execute his planned entrapment, he went into Solomon's office panting and grabbing his chest, saying he had almost fainted that morning, felt nauseated, and was afraid he was having a heart attack. He took Dennis Zawodni along to witness his performance.

After he looked in the stranger's eyes for a few seconds through the iridology lens, Solomon told him he didn't have a heart problem. "There is nothing wrong with your heart," he said, "but you do have gout, parasites in your blood, and your uric acid is high."

Dr. Merkle was intrigued by Solomon's speed and accuracy, but acted like he'd never heard of gout or uric acid before. He said, "That sounds pretty bad. What is it?"

Solomon flipped through a small card-file box sitting on his desk until he found the card titled *GOUT.* He handed it to Dr. Merkle and said, "Here, you can read this."

Dr. Merkle pretended to read the card, but after a few seconds he asked if he could take it home with him. Solomon shook his head, saying "No, you won't have any use for it."

He held out his hand, took back the card, and returned it to the card-file. The card contained a description of gout and gouty arthritis, an acute condition caused by high uric acid. It also listed herbs that would lower the uric acid in the body.

Mr. Zawodni wrote down the names of three herbs Solomon suggested Dr. Merkle might want to take to correct his problems. As they got up to leave, Dr. Merkle turned around and asked if he should continue taking his insulin.

"Oh, you have sugar?" Solomon asked in a surprised tone.

"Yes!" Dr. Merkle lied.

"No, you don't," Solomon exclaimed. "You don't have to take insulin at all." Solomon took another quick look in his eyes just to be sure. Diabetes was not there; had never been there.

When Dr. Merkle asked how much he owed him, Solomon said, "You don't owe me anything."

Dr. Merkle made it perfectly clear that he wouldn't be purchasing any herbs. Solomon calmly assured him that nobody was ever expected to buy anything. Herbs were for sale only as a convenience for those who wanted them.

With that, the imposters turned around and left.

Back in the office, Dr. Merkle wrote a scathing report of his visit to Solomon, which he presented at the next Wells County Board of Health meeting. He desperately wanted to release a story to area newspapers charging Solomon with practicing medicine without a license. He got a nod from members of the board, but since at that time the health department was housed in the Caylor-Nickel Clinic, he also had to have their approval to release the story. Permission was denied.

When that effort failed, Dr. Merkle sent a letter on his official health department letterhead to the Indiana State Board of Health in Indianapolis full of accusations that Solomon Wickey was practicing medicine without a license.

He also arranged for an old crony who worked there to send a standard, formal complaint form to Dennis Zawodni. Zawodni, acting not in his official capacity, but as a private citizen, filled out the form and sent it to the Indiana Attorney General – consumer protection division, charging Solomon Wickey with practicing medicine without a license.

But their skullduggery turned out to be nothing more than an exercise in futility, because when the attorney general's office passed the complaint back to Solomon's home county, the Adams County prosecuting attorney once again refused to take legal action. Solomon Wickey had a huge following. Even if the accusations had seemed somewhat legitimate, bringing legal charges against Solomon Wickey would have been political suicide for any man seeking election, or re-election, in Adams County.

Perhaps those two previous attempts had failed, but this time would be different. The Preacher had given them the perfect key to success: **According to Old Order Amish law, an Amish man cannot hire an attorney to defend himself.**

69

That little tidbit of information was the answer to his prayers. It would be like taking candy from a baby, because without a defense, Solomon would lose by default.

For the next ten-years, perhaps Solomon could sell a few herbs to his fellow prison inmates. All Dr. Merkle had to do was make sure the state brought formal legal charges against Solomon Wickey. Once that was done, he and the Preacher could simply sit back to wait and watch.

The vindictive little scheme was set in motion when a young teenager named Penny was admitted to emergency care at the Caylor-Nickel Hospital suffering from a complication of sugar diabetes. She had been a patient of one of the pediatricians at Caylor-Nickel Clinic for some length of time through Crippled Children's Services, and was well-known there.

One of the emergency room nurses whispered to Dr. Merkle that Penny mentioned her uncle had taken her to see Solomon Wickey a few weeks earlier, and the nurse thought she remembered the girl saying he told her to stop taking insulin.

Red Alert! Red Alert! Quick, call Dennis Zawodni, the sewer inspector turned master sleuth.

Zawodni didn't waste a minute. Instead of waiting until the girl got home from school to begin his investigation, he ran right over to the high school. Before the assistant principal would call the girl out of class, he insisted on asking the mother for permission to speak to her daughter. The mother was hesitant when he called, but after Zawodni impressed her with the urgency of the matter, she reluctantly agreed.

Penny was called to the assistant principal's office for the interrogation. Frightened out of her wits and painfully embarrassed by being called to *the office,* she had little to say beyond the fact

70

that, yes, her uncle had taken her to see Solomon Wickey. Her uncle bought an herb Mr. Wickey had suggested, which she said she threw away. However, she said, she didn't recall that Mr. Wickey mentioned, or discussed, insulin.

Undaunted by her lack of cooperation, Dr. Merkle straightaway contacted Bob Murray at the Indiana State Board of Health in Indianapolis to demand a full investigation of Solomon Wickey. After all, practicing medicine without a license is FRAUD; a criminal act that requires thorough examination.

Meanwhile, back in Adams County, things were going along pretty much as usual at Solomon's place…with one exception. A few of the Preacher's overly zealous supporters took great pleasure in peppering Solomon with a barrage of homespun dirty tricks.

One night all of the doors on Solomon's barn were mysteriously opened. Halters were unbuckled and removed, encouraging livestock to cause a huge ruckus in a midnight romp around the barnyard.

Another night, pasture gates were thrown wide open and securely wired against fence posts, so livestock could trample several acres of Solomon's corn struggling to stay alive during the drought.

Yet another night, fences were cut with wire cutters, and fence-wire was pulled aside to create an opening large enough to drive his cattle and horses, including the Standardbreds, out into the middle of the county road, and beyond, causing Solomon to have to pay crop damage to his neighbor. He and his sons spent the next several days repairing fences and rounding up their horses and livestock.

On another occasion, as two of the Wickey boys walked into the feedlot behind the barn just before dark one evening to feed the calves, they surprised three grown men standing against the barn in the shadows. One wore glasses. All three wore rather short, dark beards and black broad brimmed hats. When the three realized they had been caught and recognized, each man, in a single frantic leap, vaulted across a four-foot fence topped by two strands of tight barbwire, leaving behind only the faint echo of flying gravel as they disappeared into the growing darkness.

Were these unprovoked assaults the result of a petty little chickenshit war some of the Preacher's more rabid followers had declared against Solomon; a war they intended to fight with an endless bombardment of despicable, dirty tricks? Or were the tricks merely a cowardly, underhanded way of trying to run Solomon out of the neighborhood? If so, why? Because he stood for truth and honesty? Because they suspected he made too much money? Because he spoke out against the Preacher's transgressions? Or was there possibly a less obvious reason?

Was there not one man among them with enough courage to discuss his difference of opinion with Solomon, man to man, in an honorable way according to Amish law? Or could it be that this handful of *fine upstanding Amish men* were simply trying to protect their own lifestyle, since they had a lot in common with the Preacher?

Solomon, and his opinion, were both highly respected in his own church district, as well as in Old Order Amish church districts throughout Indiana and neighboring states. He was not a prude by any means. He enjoyed life and having a good time as much as the next person. However, he would be the first to admit that he didn't fit into a growing circle of more liberal-minded Amish men in his church district, because he faithfully followed God's laws. He believed in being faithful to his wife and family. He did not drink from the vine, nor did he keep a wine cellar as was the growing practice in the neighborhood.

In early childhood Solomon had given himself to God; to the teachings of Jesus Christ. For him, there could be no compromise, not even at the risk of being shunned, or cast out of the Old Order Amish brotherhood.

Solomon held fast to his beliefs and principles and in spite of the recent torment and abuse, outwardly his life went on uninterrupted. He and his family were healthy and happy. Three days a week his shop was full of people seeking help, and the United Parcel truck continued to turn into his driveway every day, as usual.

Let us not therefore judge one another any more;
But judge this rather,
That no man put a stumbling block or an occasion to fall in his
brother's way.
Romans 14:13

SEVEN

MERVIN S. WICKEY
October 6, 1981 – June 4, 1983

Wednesday, June 1, 1983 was a warm, sunny day, perfect for little boys to romp barefoot around the yard exploring every bug, every dandelion, every blade of new grass; everything.

Ervin and Mervin Wickey couldn't get enough of running first here, then there, trying to imitate their brothers, Levi and Joe, who were flip-flopping around the yard, but when they spotted their mother leaving the herb shop on her way to the house they ran to meet her with squeals of delight.

She held the small hand of each, one in her right hand, one in her left, as they walked up the sidewalk together. Ervin was perfectly happy walking with her, but Mervin was unusually rambunctious that day. He tugged and tugged until finally, when they were about half way to the back door, she allowed his little hand to pull away so he could run through the grass to play with Joe and Levi. Anna Mae, with Ervin in tow, hurried on into the house to fix lunch.

Not more than five or six minutes later, when Alvin passed through the kitchen, as hungry boys will do, Anna Mae sent him to find Mervin, because looking through the kitchen window, she couldn't see him in the yard with his brothers. For some unknown reason...call it a mother's intuition...she called after Alvin as he went out the back door, telling him to be sure to check around the horse watering tank, even though she felt certain it was a place Mervin had not yet discovered.

Barely ten minutes after Mervin had pulled away from his mother to romp in the yard, Alvin ran screaming toward the house carrying his baby brother by the suspenders, face down, just as he had plucked him from six inches of water in the horse watering tank. He was not breathing.

Edith ran to the neighbor for help as fast as she could go. Solomon came running from the shop to work on the baby. The Emergency Care Ambulance arrived only a few minutes later.

The paramedics grabbed Mervin, administered cardio pulmonary resuscitation (CPR), and hooked him to a life support machine in an effort to re-establish breathing, before heading to the Adams County Memorial Hospital in Decatur.

The emergency medical technicians refused to allow Solomon and Anna Mae to ride along, but a Good Samaritan in Solomon's waiting room volunteered to take them.

A short distance from the house, they waited about forty-five minutes as paramedics from Decatur, and EMT personnel from Berne, stopped their two rescue vehicles side by side facing each other in the middle of county road 400-S, feverishly working to save the baby's life.

Three hours after arriving at the hospital in Decatur, Mervin was transferred to the intensive care nursery unit at Lutheran Hospital in Ft. Wayne, and that time Solomon and Anna Mae were allowed to ride in the ambulance with him.

How Mervin, a short, rather small child for his age, got into the deep horse watering tank remains a mystery to this day. The bottom of the smooth metal tank set directly on the ground, and the wide rim around the top was much too high for him to reach, even if he jumped. There was nothing on the ground around the tank for him to climb up on, not even a small stone. It was an accident without explanation!

After four days, having done everything they could to save his life, doctors at Lutheran Hospital took Mervin off life support hoping he would be able to continue breathing on his own. But it was not to be.

Solomon and Anna Mae spent every minute of the four days at his side, waiting, hoping, praying, but sadly, with the heart-wrenching sorrow known only by a parent losing a child, they had to say good-bye to their precious young son and let him go.

He was twenty months old.

EIGHT

By mid-July, 1983, Dr. Merkle's letter of complaint against Solomon Wickey had worked its way up the ladder of Indiana state government, through the department of health to the consumer protection division of the attorney general's office, and finally landed on the desk of Michael Minglin, the consumer protection division's assistant director.

Minglin, a young opportunist with very little actual experience, was bent upon making a name for himself. Prosecuting a sure-to-win, high profile case in which the medical establishment took aim at an Amish man unable to defend himself held great promise for accomplishing that end. At least it would be a rather significant first step.

Through Janet Wiley, a law clerk in his office, Michael Minglin contacted John T. Shettle, Superintendent of the Indiana State Police, to request an official investigation of Solomon Wickey. In turn, a directive was sent to Captain Robert Burns at the Indiana State Police Post in Ft. Wayne. Captain Burns assigned the task to Detective Sergeant Robyn A. Wiley, a seasoned criminal investigator.

Sergeant Wiley immediately went to Indianapolis for a strategy planning meeting with Michael Minglin and Janet Wiley to make certain the investigation would produce the results they desired.

The official investigation began the next day with a visit to Wells County Sanitarian, Dennis Zawodni, to inquire about his previous investigation, as well as to discuss the complaint he filed with the consumer protection division of the attorney general's office in which he accused Solomon J. Wickey of practicing medicine without a license. However, Sergeant Wiley saw no need to contact the Adams County sheriff, the Adams County prosecutor, or anyone else with a more positive attitude about Solomon Wickey and the service he performed.

It was Sergeant Wiley's intention to storm the castle, so to speak, by making a surprise visit to Solomon Wickey, so on the morning of July 28, he pulled his unmarked car into Solomon's driveway and parked in front of the herb shop. A young lad stopped him as he walked toward the front door, to ask what he wanted. Wiley said he was there to see Solomon Wickey. The boy, Solomon's son, told him the office was closed that day.

When Wiley insisted on making an appointment for the next day, a female voice from inside the building responded through an open window, saying the first available appointment was one week later, on August 4th, but if it was urgent, he could come back the next day and wait his turn.

On the morning of July 29, Detective Sergeant Robyn A. Wiley again went out to Solomon Wickey's place accompanied by Indiana State Police Detective, Dennis Guillaumes, driving a separate surveillance unit.

It was a high level raid, of sorts. Wiley was wired with a body transmitter being monitored by Guillaumes, who was parked more than a mile away. Guillaumes was instructed to observe, and note, all traffic heading toward the Wickey place, while he stood ready to spring into action to assist with an arrest.

Wiley sat in the waiting room observing everybody, everything, for about two hours. Finally, when he was face to face with Solomon in his back room office, he made a point of addressing him as "Doctor Wickey." He introduced himself as Rob Wilkins, and launched into his well-rehearsed spiel.

He told Solomon that after a series of exhausting tests, his doctor had diagnosed him as a diabetic, and had prescribed the drug, Orinase, to be taken on a regular basis. He went on to say that six months later his doctor told him the diabetes was getting worse and he would have to go on insulin. But, he said, before doing so he wanted a second opinion.

Solomon picked up the iridology glass, studied his right eye for five or six seconds, and repeated the process with his left eye.

"You definitely don't have diabetes," he said, "but you do have a heart problem, and worms in your pancreas. Did you know that?"

"Well, no I didn't," Wiley replied.

"Yes, you do!" Solomon declared as he jotted the name of three herbs on a piece of blank note paper.

"You can tell all of that by just looking in my eyes?"

Solomon nodded, saying the eyes are the window of the body. He flipped through a well-used iridology book lying on his desk until he found a diagram of an iris showing a similar problem, pointed it out to his visitor, then closed the book and laid it aside.

Solomon handed the note paper bearing the names of the herbs to Wiley, and on his way out the detective purchased all three; golden seal, safflower and black walnut for $19.67.

When he returned to the office, Sergeant Wiley placed the note paper Solomon had given him, along with the herbs he purchased, into the evidence vault at the State Police Post in Ft. Wayne for safe keeping.

His report was exactly what Michael Mingling and Janet Wiley wanted. In it, Wiley stated, unequivocally, that Solomon Wickey was practicing medicine. He pointed out that he had never had a problem with his heart, and when Solomon said he did, that was definitely a diagnosis. He also stated that he felt certain Solomon only showed him the iridology book to impress him with the fact that medical doctors were using the same technique to diagnose, because the guy who wrote it had *"doctor"* in front of his name. Little did it matter to the detective that the iridology book in question was written by Bernard Jensen, D.C., Nutritionist, not a medical doctor.

Another point Sergeant Wiley used to support his opinion was a conversation he overheard between two couples in the waiting room. It seemed as though the wife of the couple from Terre Haute, Indiana, started seeing Solomon soon after undergoing open heart surgery six months before. Wiley avowed that she said Solomon had replaced medications prescribed by her doctor with herbs. He stated that she told the other couple the doctor had recently prescribed aspirin to thin her blood, but she refused to take it until she got a nod from Solomon.

Later, when they were in Solomon's office, Sergeant Wiley reported that he could hear a muffled conversation between the Terre Haute couple and someone with a shrill, high-pitched voice, which he believed to be that of Solomon Wickey, telling her not to take the aspirin, take herbs instead.

Sergeant Wiley filed his written report with Captain Burns in Ft. Wayne, who in turn, forwarded a copy to Michael Minglin and Janet Wiley. Based on that report, they immediately proceeded with plans to bring legal charges against Solomon Wickey for practicing medicine without a license.

On Tuesday afternoon, the 6th day of September, 1983, Michael Minglin called Max Coburn, their investigator. He asked Coburn to go to Berne to inform Solomon Wickey of the attorney general's intention to petition the Adams County Circuit Court to issue a restraining order to close his place of business in order to prevent him from continuing the unlawful practice of medicine. Coburn was also instructed to observe everything going on at that location, and to file a detailed report with Minglin immediately upon his return to Indianapolis.

Coburn drove to Berne the next morning. He pulled in alongside eight or ten vehicles parked in Solomon's driveway, got out, and went inside where he observed a young Amish woman, immaculate in her traditional light blue summer dress, sparkling white cap and apron, working behind the sales counter.

He took it as a personal affront when she seemed much too busy with a stack of paper and a calculator to acknowledge him when he entered the room. In fact, nobody in the room spoke to him, so after standing for a couple of minutes, he quietly took a seat alongside others who were waiting.

Eventually, a man came out of a room somewhere behind the sales counter, and handed the young woman a piece of paper. Still she did not speak. She took several bottles off the back shelf and set them on the counter, clicked buttons on her calculator, and told him

83

that would be $64.80. He paid in cash, made another appointment, and left.

Without a word, two women... apparently the next appointment...got up and went toward the back of the building, evidently to Wickey's examining room.

Still, nobody paid any attention to him. Max Coburn absolutely hated being ignored, but this was an official surveillance, so instead of flashing his badge and causing a scene, he continued sitting there trying to discern what was going on in the back room. At one point, even though the voices were barely audible, he thought he heard Doctor Wickey say, "This is badly ulcerated." He had no proof the voice was actually that of Solomon Wickey. It was only a subjective evaluation.

The two women came out a few minutes later and handed a piece of paper to the young woman behind the counter. "Dad, we don't have this," she called out.

A bearded man, whom Coburn assumed to be Solomon Wickey, came from the back of the building, happily whistling as he walked through the waiting room and went outside toward a stack of corrugated boxes the United Parcel driver had just delivered. The two women followed him.

It was the chance Coburn had been waiting for. He got up, walked to the door, and stood in the doorway observing from a distance, but didn't follow them outside. Instead, he watched as Solomon tore into one of the boxes, took out a small package, and handed it to one of the women.

Yes, in deedy, there was absolutely no question about it. Michael Minglin was justified in charging Solomon Wickey with practicing medicine. He personally had caught the man red-handed. Wickey used the word *ulcerated.* That was a diagnosis. Then with

84

his own eyes he saw Wickey hand medication to the woman. A shut and closed case!

Investigator Coburn made no effort to speak to the women or to determine the contents of the package. His mind was made up. Little did it matter that the package contained plant fertilizer for the Miller Sisters' flowers.

As soon as the two women left, Coburn walked outside and said, "Doctor Wickey, can I speak to you in private?"

Solomon didn't respond. He simply led the way into the nearby buggy shed.

Coburn took great pleasure in flashing his badge, as he told Solomon he was there to inform him the Indiana Attorney General intended to ask the Adams County Circuit Court judge to issue a restraining order to prevent him from practicing medicine without a license.

"You don't have a medical license, do you?"

"No." Solomon was dumbfounded. He sold herbs, not drugs, he reasoned silently, so how could anyone accuse him of practicing medicine?

Sure enough, about mid-morning on Friday, September 9, 1983, an Adams County deputy sheriff knocked on Solomon's door to deliver the temporary restraining order issued by Judge Robert Anderson less than an hour before.

The restraining order stated that Solomon's place of business would be closed until September 30, 1983, at which time a hearing would be held before the Adams County Circuit Court to decide if the restraining order should be made permanent.

Michael Minglin had convinced the judge to issue the order by saying Solomon was not only practicing medicine without a license, but was also engaged in deceptive acts and misrepresentations. He did not allege that Solomon had harmed anyone, but insisted he had been practicing medicine unlawfully by selling herbs to people from all over the country out of a small office located on his farm.

It would be untruthful to say Solomon was not hurt and dismayed as he watched the deputy slap the notice on his shop door. It is only human nature to feel a burst of outrage and humiliation when you are falsely accused, and he was no exception.

Solomon immediately called upon his unshakable faith by turning this hurtful situation over to God, knowing full-well that if it was His will for this work to continue, He would provide the way.

Once he had given the burden to God, Solomon and his sons peacefully went about the business of taking care of the farm and shucking what little corn their land produced in spite of the drought.

*****

When people began arriving at Solomon's place on Monday morning only to find the shop closed with a temporary restraining order posted on the door, telephones began to ring!

By mid-week several people had called the corporate offices of Nature's Sunshine in Utah, and PURE HERBS, LTD in Michigan. They recited the charges, and said Solomon was helpless, since, according to Amish law, he could not hire a lawyer to defend himself. Therefore, he was facing a long prison sentence, along with a stiff fine, if help wasn't forthcoming. Solomon's loyal supports hadn't yet learned that the ball was already rolling.

Andrew David Harrison was eager to meet his company's new Distributor #1, and as fate would have it, he drove down to Berne with Dr. Watkins the day after Solomon's herb shop was closed by court order to make his acquaintance.

As soon as he got home, Harrison immediately called PURE HERBS, LTD.'s outside counsel, Kirkpatrick W. Dilling, the senior partner in the very prestigious Chicago law firm, Dilling, Dilling and Gronek, for help and advice. Dilling recommended Jerrald Crowell, a well known attorney in Ft. Wayne, to act as Solomon's local defense attorney.

Harrison called Crowell. He agreed to take the case. A few days later, as soon as Crowell concluded a trial already in progress, he and Harrison went to Berne to meet with Solomon. Of course, Solomon couldn't hire either of them, but when the matter of payment for his defense came up, he told them Nature's Sunshine provided a legal assistance program for their distributors.

Kirkpatrick W. Dilling, who also acted as the outside counsel for Nature's Sunshine, took care of all the financial details. In addition, he assigned Robert Armstrong to Solomon's case.

Andrew David Harrison, who was not only a partner in PURE HERBS LTD., but also a lawyer of some repute, volunteered his services as part of the defense team, saying that for Solomon Wickey, he would work free.

When Bob Black just happened to go to Berne a few days after the deputy sheriff's visit, Solomon told him what was going on. Once Bob got back to Ft. Wayne he made a few phone calls himself, and it didn't take long to find out that somebody had hired a local ace, Jerrald Crowell, to defend Solomon.

Bob knew Crowell personally, and called him the next day offering to help. He explained that he and Solomon had been best friends for several years, and even though Solomon couldn't say anything to defend himself, he most likely could tell them whatever they needed to know on Solomon's behalf.

Early the next week the defense team had begun to organize. Time was short. September 30 was only a few days away. It was decided that Andrew David Harrison would act as the general counsel, Robert Armstrong would act as the research counsel, and Jerrald Crowell would act as the trial counsel.

On September 22nd, Jerrald Crowell filed paperwork with the Adams County Circuit Court notifying them that he, along with Robert Armstrong and Andrew David Harrison, would appear as co-counsel for the defendant, Solomon J. Wickey. He told the judge that Andrew David Harrison was a leading expert in the field of differentiating between nutritional consultation and practicing medicine without a license, and Robert Armstrong was an expert on legal technicalities in this field.

He also filed a motion asking for a continuance, because, he said, he had not been retained to defend Solomon Wickey until September 20, and couldn't appear at 9:00 A.M. on September 30, because of a previously scheduled hearing in the Allen County Superior Court that morning.

Due to the complexities of the issues involved, Crowell also filed a motion asking the court for an extension of time to conduct an investigation of the state's allegations.

The court granted permission for the out-of-state attorneys, Armstrong and Harrison, to participate as part of Solomon's defense team, and set the hearing on Crowell's motion for extension of time for 9:30 A.M. on the 30th day of September, 1983.

The clerk of the Adams County Circuit Court dutifully sent a certified copy of the motions, and the court's rulings, to each attorney involved. Michael Minglin was shocked to learn Solomon Wickey was being defended…and by a team of very expensive, well-known attorneys, no less. His plans for greatness abruptly went awry, because the heretofore defenseless Amish pushover had suddenly become a solid granite mountain.

In the meantime, hundreds of Solomon's staunch supporters wrote letters of protest to Judge Robert Anderson, demanding that *ALL* charges against Solomon Wickey be dropped. Among other things, they said:

> It is each person's constitutional right to choose how they take care of their own body, and there is no law that says they have to consult a medical doctor.

> If someone says they have a headache and you suggest they take two aspirin and go to bed, you are just as guilty of practicing medicine in the State of Indiana as Solomon Wickey.

> Solomon Wickey has a special God-given gift. Obviously a medical license was not one of God's requirements when He bestowed the gift.

> A court of law cannot usurp a Divine mandate.

> When is the Indiana Attorney General going after Christian Science Practitioners? They don't have a medical license.

A few days before his court date, Bob Black picked Solomon up and took him to Ft. Wayne for a preliminary meeting with Jerrald Crowell. Even in this critical situation, Solomon held fast to his refusal to say anything against his fellow man. When Crowell asked him a question that required a derogatory comment about someone, Solomon looked at Bob, then remained silent while Bob answered the question. Without the free exchange between Jerrald Crowell and Bob Black, Solomon could not have been adequately represented before the court.

The stage was set. People began arriving at the Adams County Courthouse in Decatur, Indiana, before seven o'clock on the morning of September 30, 1983. LOTS of people!

Four men showed up with an ample supply of a small, colorful booklet titled *Citizens Rule Book...The Bill of Rights and Jury Handbook* generously donated by John Broomall, a Wickey supporter from Ohio. Two of the four gentlemen stood at the front entrance to the courthouse, two at the back entrance, and handed a booklet to everyone as they walked in, as well as to those who stood in the yard outside when standing room was no longer available in the courtroom, or in the adjoining hallways. It was a record-setting crowd, far beyond anything the tiny Adams County Courthouse had experienced before. Even the jury box was filled with spectators.

Inside the courtroom the judicial process began. Michael Minglin, a rather short, thin, wispy, young man, along with his law clerk, Janet Wiley, took their places at the prosecutor's table.

Jerrald Crowell, a mature, well-known and highly respected attorney in both Allen and Adams Counties, and Andrew David Harrison, the tall, well-built, red-headed attorney from Michigan, strolled into the courtroom a couple of minutes later to take their seats at the defense table. The defendant was not with them, because, according to Amish law, Solomon could not voluntarily present himself there. The court would have to order him to be seated up front.

At precisely 9:30 Judge Robert Anderson, dressed in his black judicial robes, rapped his gavel to call the court to order. He started by saying he was thrilled, and amazed, to see so many of the electorate in the audience. (He was running for election). He estimated that more than 250 people were crammed into that small room.

The judge told the crowd that so far he had received more than 225 letters, with a new stack arriving daily, all supportive of Solomon Wickey. Nearly every letter, he said, bore thirty to forty signatures.

He took a few minutes to explain the legal process, and address the misunderstandings people seemed to have about the case. For instance, he said, his was a court of the people. He explained that this was a civil suit, not a criminal matter, nor was Mr. Wickey ever under arrest, as many people thought. The judge continued by saying the case was not brought by the Adams County Court, but was filed in that court by the State of Indiana.

In reply to many of the letters he had received, Judge Anderson stated that Indiana law does not make it a crime for one person to tell another to take an aspirin. Such advice, he said, is not considered practicing medicine, therefore is not prohibited under the law.

Solomon was seated in the back of the room with Anna Mae and a few close friends and relatives. With a nod from the judge, attorney Harrison went to escort Solomon to the defense table so the proceedings could begin.

The instant Solomon was on his feet, the entire audience, with the exception of four or five state witnesses, immediately stood for a very loud, resounding, ovation which Judge Anderson obviously enjoyed, and allowed to continue for several minutes before rapping for silence.

Jerrald Crowell asked the judge to rule on two motions he had filed with the court earlier. He pleaded that the motion for continuance was filed so the defense team could have time to catch up with the state attorneys who had more than a two month head start. Crowell said the defense team needed time to conduct an investigation of these complex issues, and to take depositions from several people. In his opinion, he continued, one day would not be enough to present testimony, but he thought three days would be sufficient.

Andrew David Harrison concurred. He told the judge that he'd had more than ten years experience with this type case, and assured him that they were decidedly complex issues, often involving an individual's constitutional rights.

At that point Michael Minglin jumped up to object, stating emphatically that the Wickey case was not at all complex. He pointed out that the state's witnesses were present, and the state was ready to proceed at once. The only issues were: (1) was Wickey in violation of the Indiana Medical Practices Act, and (2) was he licensed as a doctor.

Judge Anderson overruled Minglin's objection. He reasoned that the case was, indeed, complicated and Mr. Wickey was entitled to have all of those matters looked into. On that note, he granted both motions filed by the defense team.

The judge reset the case for 9:00A.M. December 1, 1983, at which time he would hear evidence for, and against, the State of Indiana's request for a permanent restraining order to keep Solomon Wickey from allegedly engaging in improper medical practice.

He advised the attorneys that his calendar was full of other pending cases, so it may not be possible to set aside three days in a row to hear this case. Thus, he said, the hearing starting on December 1st might possibly be spread over three separated days.

Judge Anderson ruled that the temporary restraining order would remain in effect until December 1, 1983.

Court was adjourned for the day.

*****

The defense team had a great deal of work to do during the next sixty days, while on the other hand, Solomon was prohibited from working at all. It was a very difficult time for him, and for his family; one that took a toll on all of them.

He and his sons completed fall harvest, repaired fences, shod the horses, and piddled around with a few odd jobs. Many English folks stopped by his house to say hello and to offer help and encouragement, but then, of course, there were also a few naysayers full of discouraging, unwanted advice.

Solomon was understandably restless, so he decided to take a trip. Why not? He and Anna Mae had been through enough recently. They might as well use this time to travel; to rebalance.

Solomon and Anna Mae invited a happy, supportive group to go along; their oldest son, David, and his bride, Sylvia, their oldest daughter, Anna Mae, Jr. and her new husband, Sam, and two of Solomon's brothers, Amos and his wife, Emma, and David and his wife, Bertha.

Solomon arranged for a large van and driver, and as soon as Anna Mae made arrangements for a relative to look after the children, they were on their way.

Fall foliage was at its peak in mid-October as they headed across northern Ohio into north central Pennsylvania for a few days visit with the Wickey brothers' sister, Lizzie, and her family. While they were in the vicinity, they also visited an Amish family that had become good friends as a result of regular trips to Solomon's office.

New York State was even more colorful than Pennsylvania had been. Their van headed to Rochester, northeast across the Allegheny Mountains, around Lake Ontario, and along the bank of the St. Lawrence River on their way to Norfolk, population 1,353, located in upper New York, a few miles south of the US-Canadian border between Massena and Potsdam.

The colorful brush strokes of nature became more awe-inspiring with each bend in the road, especially for Solomon, who, even though he had been born and raised in the flatlands, had always had a yen to live among the huge trees, rocks and rushing streams in hill country.

The Wickeys enjoyed two days and two nights with relatives and friends in, and around, Norfolk, but before leaving the region, they decided to set aside a day just to relax and explore.

They climbed to the observation deck for a look at the St. Lawrence-FDR Power Project. They crossed the Seaway International Bridge between Ontario, Canada and the United States, near Massena, New York. The highlight of the day, however, was the Dwight D. Eisenhower Locks on the St. Lawrence River. It was fascinating to stand on the viewing deck, eyes fixed on one huge ocean-going ship after another being lifted and lowered forty-two feet through the giant lock chamber on their way to, or from, Lake Ontario or the Atlantic Ocean, bearing cargo destined for world wide ports-of-call.

The next morning they headed southeast across the Adirondack Mountains, brilliantly dressed in red, green and gold, on their way to Virginia Beach and the Atlantic Ocean.

The ocean was as much of an adventure as the mountains had been. It was relaxing to do nothing but sit on the beach watching dozens of huge commercial ships, along with U.S. Navy and Coast Guard ships, arrive in the harbor, while other large vessels heading out to open sea became tiny indistinguishable specs disappearing beyond the place where the sky and ocean became one.

Colorful sailboats dipped and rolled to the rhythm of wind and wave, while bold, adventurous young men, skillfully balanced on surf boards, rode frothy, unpredictable waves alive with the roar of the breakers.

The Wickeys laughed, and splashed, and ran barefoot along the beach at water's edge, while incoming tides stung their feet and ankles with sand, seaweed and tiny shells as seagulls soared and squalled overhead. For Amish farmers, it was a different world.

When the travelers said goodbye to the ocean the next day, they turned their attention once again to mountain scenery. In the early morning fog just ahead of sunrise, their van rolled northwestward along Interstate 64, across the very same soil where men fought and died during major battles of both the Revolutionary and Civil Wars. It was a temptation not to stop for a closer look, but one of the most picturesque mountain ranges on earth beckoned.

At Waynesboro, Virginia, their driver turned onto the Blue Ridge Parkway, a five-hundred-mile scenic byway connecting a continuous chain of high mountain peaks as it wound through the Shenandoah National Park in Virginia, and the Blue Ridge and Great Smoky Mountains in North Carolina.

Within a few hours the road, protected by strong guardrails on either side, climbed higher and higher toward the sun, as colorful deciduous trees gave way to a dense green forest filled with huge, long-needled pines oozing turpentine. The roadside marker indicated that they had left Virginia and had entered the Blue Ridge Mountain Range in North Carolina.

The driver pulled to a stop near a Swiss chalet perched on the crest of a high mountain peak at Little Switzerland, the perfect place to rest, stretch, fill their lungs with pure mountain air, bellow an authentic Swiss-German yodel or two, and listen as the sound playfully bounced from one mountain peak to another before it echoed back to the sender.

Solomon and his daughter, both accomplished yodelers, took advantage of the place, but the game of playing echo was tossed aside when the aroma of fresh, pan-fried mountain trout and hush puppies filling the air, enticed the hungry tourists to indulge.

As they headed south after lunch, the driver shifted down at the bottom of a steep incline to prevent the van from laboring unduly. Any discomfort from the increasingly higher altitude was forgotten once they reached the top where a roadside overlook provided an awesome, unspoiled view of Mount Mitchell in the distance, which at 6,684 feet above sea level, is the highest elevation in the eastern United States.

From that vantage point they looked down into a clear blue sky to watch puffy, cumulus clouds lazily drifting above a rainbow a thousand feet, or so, below. No one spoke. Each of them felt much too humble, too insignificant, standing there among the clouds on what is said to be the oldest mountains in the world, where the reverence of the place pays tribute to the powerful, all encompassing presence of the Creator.

By next sunrise the Wickeys, fully rested after a good night's sleep, were on their way again. Having exited the Blue Ridge Parkway at Asheville, North Carolina, they drove west on U.S. 40, reluctantly leaving the majestic Blue Ridge and Great Smoky Mountains behind.

The trip through Tennessee was somewhat uneventful, but at the first sight of Standardbred horses grazing in a pasture near the outskirts of Lexington, Kentucky, Solomon became excited. He directed the driver to leave the interstate highway in favor of a secondary road between Lexington and Versailles, a scenic route past the famous Keeneland Race Track, where some of his own colts sired by Leonard A. had stood in the winner's circle. For several miles, they drove past huge, impressive, well maintained horse farms in the heart of The Bluegrass, home to thousands of Standardbreds and Thoroughbreds alike. Solomon wanted to stop and look around, but Anna Mae was eager to get back to the children.

Their last night away from home was spent in southern Indiana with another Wickey brother who lived near Salem.

It had been a wonderful, most enjoyable trip; one each of them would long remember. Two weeks after leaving, they were back in Adams County ready to confront whatever challenges the future held.

Opinion

Richard G. Inskeep
President and Publisher

Craig Klugman
Editor

Tim Harmon
Managing Editor

Larry J. Hayes
Opinion Page Editor

The Journal-Gazette   Tuesday, October 18, 1983

Whose medicine is no good?

We want to discuss the case of Solomon J. Wickey. He's the farmer in Adams County who gives neighbors and, in fact, people throughout the area advice about how herbs can cure their aches and pains.

Apparently, nobody says Wickey's counsel ever hurt anybody; a lot of people swear by his home remedies. He doesn't charge anything, although he accepts modest donations. He calls it nutritional counseling. But the Indiana attorney general's office calls it practicing medicine without a license, and has taken him to court in a civil complaint to get Wickey to stop what he does.

The judge in the case has issued a temporary restraining order, which means Wickey isn't supposed to be giving out his nutritional advice. Early this month, the judge agreed to delay the trial until Dec. 1. So there is the basic outline of the case, and, frankly, we are puzzled.

It's hard to understand just why the attorney general's office has decided to bring the full power of the state of Indiana against Wickey. You have to ask yourself *just* how Wickey's herbal cures differ from chicken soup or how they are such a threat to the public wellbeing that he must be brought before a judge and maybe have to pay a fine or go to jail.

Just the other day, a local doctor was telling us horror stories about a colleague. The doctor is very uneasy about the second practitioner, and suggests he is a menace to the public health, or worse. But, alas, doctors, we're told, protect their own; the alcoholics, the incompetent, the excessively mercenary. It's rare indeed even for a local medical

society to dissociate itself from a practitioner who is thus regarded. Ever rarer is it that the state prosecutes a physician for practicing demonstrably bad medicine.

Don't get us wrong. We're not trying to egg the doctors into a controversy over regulation of the medical profession. Our impression, however, is that of the people purporting to offer cures of one sort or another, herbalist Wickey has to be very far down on the public enemy list, if he qualifies at all.

And it's not as if Indiana has never demonstrated a certain liberality toward exotic medical treatments. Consider that the state was the second in the country to approve Laetrile, used in the treatment of cancer but of no proven benefit, except perhaps to growers of apricots, from whose pits the drug is derived.

The very worst that can be said for Wickey is that his herbs surely are no more dangerous than Laetrile. In both instances, it seems more a problem that by turning to folk medicine, people aren't getting the treatment modern medicine could offer.

One final word. That thousands of people look to people like Wickey for treatment is a rather eloquent statement about their attitude toward the miracles of modern medicine. It simply has become so arcane and complex that it's beyond understanding of many people. Doctors talk mumbo-jumbo, and it just turns off some people. They look for alternatives, such as Wickey. Which brings us to the really sad thing about this present case: Medicine can't cure the first blister if the patient doesn't trust the physician.

NINE

Thursday, December 1, 1983, dawned cold and bleak. However, the dreary weather did not discourage more than three hundred supporters from finding their way to Decatur, Indiana to stand solidly behind Solomon on this, the first day of testimony in his trial.

Before daybreak, sidewalks stretching two blocks in every direction were filled with men and women hurrying toward the town square to join others congregated outside the Adams County Courthouse waiting for the doors to open. Most carried small coolers or sack lunches to protect their seat in the courtroom for the entire day, if they were lucky enough to get a seat in the first place.

Gently falling snow added to the festival-like atmosphere as people milled around, some greeting friends, while others watched radio and television network news trucks filled with cameras and technical equipment jockey for a place to park, or squeeze between horses and buggies already tied to parking meters on the courthouse square.

This trial had turned into a major story. Not only was it unusual for a quiet, soft-spoken Amish man to be charged with any kind of crime, it was even more unusual to have three very prominent lawyers defend him and hundreds of people from several states lend their support by attending each day of his trial. Curious television reporters mingled with the crowd outside the building, interviewing as many people as possible, since their cameras were not allowed inside Judge Anderson's courtroom.

Andrew David Harrison, who had arrived early, seated himself at the defense table, spreading paperwork out for a last minute look while he waited for Jerrald Crowell. A stately looking gentleman, one of Solomon's staunch supporters, approached the defense table with his hand outstretched to introduce himself to Harrison, and offer a few words of encouragement. After a brief exchange, the gentleman turned to go back to his seat, but on second thought, he said, "By the way, did you know the Indiana Medical Practices law was recently re-numbered?"

"No, I didn't know that!" Harrison exclaimed. "Thank you for telling me."

Harrison turned his attention to Jerrald Crowell coming into the courtroom loaded down with manila folders, a couple of law books, and a briefcase, all of which he deposited on the defense table. He told Crowell what the gentleman had said about the statute being re-numbered, and said, "Do you think we can do anything with that?"

Crowell wasn't aware of the re-numbering, but wasted no time in sending Harrison to consult the law clerk in the judge's office. She confirmed that it had been re-numbered July 1, 1982.

The clock struck nine as Andrew David Harrison slid back into his chair at the defense table only moments before the court bailiff entered the courtroom to cry: "Everyone rise. The Adams Circuit Court is now in session to hear case number C-83-224, the

State of Indiana vs Solomon J. Wickey; Judge Robert S. Anderson presiding."

From his perch on the bench, Judge Anderson looked out over another overwhelmingly pro-Wickey, standing-room-only audience. He opened by issuing a strong warning to the various media reporters in the room that there would be NO pictures taken of Solomon Wickey, nor of his family, nor of any Amish person in the courthouse or on the grounds.

He explained to those assembled that this was a bench trial before a judge sitting without a jury. Therefore, the final decision would be made by the presiding judge. The number of letters he had received from Wickey supporters, he said, exceeded four-hundred at the last count, each with forty or more signatures. He went on to say each letter appealed for dismissal of the charges against Solomon Wickey because he'd helped each of them immensely, and had harmed no one. "I have not received one letter where the writer was critical of Wickey," he said.

Judge Anderson repeated the statements he made at the beginning of the trial on September 30, to clarify any misunderstandings the audience might have, by stating that this was not a criminal case, nor had Mr. Wickey been arrested or jailed as some people erroneously believed.

At the conclusion of his opening remarks Judge Anderson asked attorney Harrison to escort Mr. Wickey to the defense table so the proceedings could begin. As Solomon walked to the front of the room beside Harrison the audience erupted into a long, boisterous, round of applause, which the judge allowed to continue for three or four minutes before he cut it off with a chop of his hand, followed by the rap of his gavel.

Immediately after the court was called to order, Michael Minglin approached the bench to submit a *verified petition for injunction,* asking the court to make the temporary restraining order permanent. It was a lengthy document in which Mr. Minglin set forth the many accusations against Solomon Wickey, saying he was guilty of:

- Holding himself out to the public as being engaged in diagnosis.
- Suggesting, recommending, and prescribing treatment for the relief, cure or prevention of the physical, mental, or functional ailment or defect of a person.
- Maintaining an office for examination and treatment.
- Attaching the designation of "Doctor" to his name.
- Defendant, Solomon Wickey, without a license, or exemption to do so, has been, and is, engaged in the practice of medicine or osteopathic medicine in the State of Indiana in violation of the law.

As soon as Mr. Minglin sat down, Jerrald Crowell approached the bench to present a *motion to dismiss.* He told the judge, "The defendant moves the court to dismiss this action because the prosecution's complaint fails to state a claim against the defendant upon which relief can be granted, in that the statute upon which said complaint is based is unconstitutionally overbroad and vague."

He went on to say, "There is not only an issue of over-breadth in connection with the statute, but there would also appear to be one as to vagueness, as is noted by the definition of diagnose or diagnosis. It would be impossible for the ordinary person to know when they were in violation of the statute, as can be seen from the following examples:

> What is *treatment, correction or prevention of other conditions of human beings* as set forth in this law? Does this apply to a manicurist working with cuticles, barbers or beauty operators working with unruly hair, or masseurs or masseuses taking the cramps out of the body muscles? In the same paragraph, does the *penetration of the body orifice by any means, for the intended palliation, relief of any physical, mental or functional ailment or defect of any person* mean that sexual intercourse outside the family in order to satisfy someone's libido, which would be a mental or physical state, would be practicing medicine? Has this become a Class C. Felony?"

Mr. Crowell's lengthy motion also quoted points of law along with the citation of several pertinent precedent cases.

The judge took each motion under advisement before he proceeded to hear the case by asking Mr. Minglin for his opening statement.

Even though Michael Minglin felt intimidated by the unexpected, overwhelming support for the defendant, he jumped right into his opening statement by saying, **"It is not the nature of evidence, it's only the seriousness of the charge that requires investigation."**

He nervously paced the floor waving an open law book, and pointed his index finger at Solomon and Judge Anderson as he aggressively asserted that the case was very simple, with just two things to decide: (1) Did Solomon Wickey perform certain acts which are directly medical, and (2) was he licensed by the state to be a doctor.

He said the state would show that Wickey did diagnose a specific ailment for a person and prescribed an herbal remedy for the illness. This, he said, was in direct violation of the state statute. He called the issue a "very serious matter," and pointed out that the legislature had designated who can, and who cannot, practice medicine in the State of Indiana. "The law is very specific!" he exclaimed.

Minglin made every effort to avoid the hard, cold stares of this critical, defiant audience as he walked back to the prosecution's table at the end of his opening statement.

In his opening statement, Jerrald Crowell recited the exemption clause in the Indiana Medical Practices Act, which he said, applied to Solomon Wickey.

It exempts any member of any church practicing its religious tenets as long as he does not make a medical diagnosis, prescribe, or administer drugs or medicine, perform surgical or physical operations, nor assume the title of, or hold himself out to be a physician.

He said the defense would show that Solomon Wickey did not prescribe drugs or medicine, but acted only as a nutritional counselor. He told the court that Wickey did not diagnose, because diagnosing refers to a patient-doctor relationship, and Solomon Wickey did not represent himself as a doctor.

"There will be no evidence to prove the defendant gave any medical diagnosis," he shouted, "nor did he sell medicine or drugs."

Crowell continued, saying that the defendant, Solomon Wickey, is of the Amish faith and interprets the language of the Bible literally. The evidence will show he was only following a religious tenet in his counseling. "Solomon believes the Bible directed him

104

to do what he does. He lives and breathes the word of God and the teachings of Jesus Christ. He is God's tool; a man with a God-given gift. **What's on trial here is not the man, Solomon Wickey, but the word of God and the teachings of Jesus Christ!"**

At that point Crowell picked up a King James Bible and waved it in the air. The audience went wild! They jumped to their feet for another lengthy, earsplitting ovation, which the judge allowed to continue for several minutes. Finally, he rapped his gavel to quiet the room, and told the audience the court preferred they not cheer like that.....but stopped short of reprimanding them.

With opening arguments for both sides concluded, Judge Anderson instructed Mr. Minglin to call his first witness for the state.

Minglin called Robert Murray.

Jerrald Crowell yelled, "I object, Your Honor. Mr. Murray is not included on the witness list we received from the prosecution, and has not been deposed."

The judge sustained the objection and excused the witness, much to the chagrin of Michael Minglin. The audience robustly applauded the decision.

The first witness to actually take the stand for the state was Dennis Zawodni. In response to Minglin's questions, Zawodni told the court his age and education, and when asked about his employment, he said he was sanitarian for the Wells County Health Department.

He testified that the investigation of Solomon Wickey began after the Wells County Health Department received a complaint from a citizen. He said he called the Indiana State Department of Health in Indianapolis about the matter, and they instructed him to investigate Wickey.

As soon as Zawodni began to tell of his personal visit to Solomon Wickey's place in 1980, Crowell yelled, "Objection, Your Honor!"

When the judge asked on what grounds, Crowell explained that his client was charged under the re-numbered statute which became law on July 1, 1982, and the witness was giving testimony about events that took place prior to that date; before this statute became law. Crowell continued by asking that all evidence prior to the re-numbering of this law be excluded from the trial.

Judge Anderson nodded in agreement as he ruled, "Objection sustained." He cautioned Minglin by saying, "Your witnesses' testimony must relate to events occurring after July 1, 1982. Is that clear?"

Michael Minglin immediately asked for a recess to collect his composure. That ruling had sent the majority of his case against Solomon Wickey down the drain because of a technicality he had foolishly overlooked. The situation was indeed grave. He felt ill.

He held his head in his thin, bony hands and sat there at the prosecution table with his eyes closed, rocking back and forth, back and forth, trying to figure out what to do. They were less than thirty minutes into the trial and already there had been two loud, cheering ovations for the defense, while, in turn, he had lost two of his most compelling witnesses. He realized that most, if not all, up-coming testimony for the state would have to be excluded. The embarrassment of the situation was agonizing. Things were definitely not going as he had planned.

His rocking back and forth, his self-indulged commiseration, was interrupted when a sudden, resounding blow struck the table in front of him. He opened one eye a slit, only to see a huge clenched fist resting there. His gaze slowly traveled from the fist up a large, muscular arm and shoulder, past a short, dark beard, and into two of the most forceful, determined steel-blue eyes he'd every seen.

Jerrald Crowell and Andrew David Harrison watched in awe from the defense table across the isle as they heard the mountain of a man tell Minglin in a very husky, stern voice, "If Solomon Wickey spends even one hour in jail, you're gonna be dealin' with me!" After making his point, he simply turned around and walked away.

Minglin froze. He wrapped his arms around his shoulders, laid his chin on his chest, and continued rocking back and forth, back and forth.

When the court re-convened after the recess Michael Minglin called Detective Sergeant Robyn A. Wiley as his next witness.

After he was sworn in, Minglin spent a few minutes asking basic questions to establish Wiley as a reputable witness in this case. In response, Wiley told the court that he lived in Ft. Wayne, Indiana, and had been employed by the Indiana State Police for ten years, the last five as a detective sergeant assigned to the criminal investigation section.

Robyn Wiley testified that the assignment to investigate Solomon Wickey came from the attorney general's office, and in reply to Minglin's interrogation, an account of his visit to Wickey's herb shop on July 29, 1983, began to unfold.

Wickey was not there the first time he went, so he went back the next day, and waited his turn, during which time, he said, "A lot of people came in and out."

Sergeant Wiley also told the court that while he waited, he observed two couples in particular who were sitting in the waiting room. He overheard one of the men say they were from Terre Haute, and that his wife, sitting beside him, had had open heart surgery approximately six months before, meaning before July 29, 1983. The man said they started coming to Doctor Wickey as soon as she was able to travel after the surgery, and in that six months he had taken her off of the medication her doctors had prescribed, and placed her on herbs instead. He went on to say that recently her doctor told her to take aspirin to thin her blood, but she wouldn't take it until Doctor Wickey said it was OK.

After the couple from Terre Haute went into the backroom office, Wiley continued, he could hear their voices, and heard Doctor Wickey tell her not to take the aspirin. She should take vitamins instead.

In response to Minglin's questioning, Wiley described the building inside and out, as well as Solomon's office area, which he referred to as his examining room. He said that when he finally went into Wickey's examining room he introduced himself as Rob Wilkins, and addressed the man as Doctor Wickey. He continued, saying that he told Doctor Wickey he had been diagnosed as a diabetic and had been prescribed the drug Orinase to take on a regular basis. After six months, his doctor said the diabetes was getting worse and he would have to go on insulin, but before doing so, he wanted a second opinion.

He said Doctor Wickey immediately said, "Don't take the insulin. It's not good for you. Don't take it." Wiley said Doctor Wickey told him the Orinase was probably what was causing his blood sugar to be high.

Wiley testified that Doctor Wickey had three magnifying glasses laying on his desk. He picked up one of them, and using a penlight, looked into his right eye for about five seconds, into the left eye for the same length of time, then said, "You definitely don't have diabetes, but you do have a slight heart problem. Did you know that?"

Wiley said he replied, "Well, no, I didn't."

"Do you have a heart problem?" Minglin asked.

"No! No, I do not!" Wiley declared emphatically.

He told the court Doctor Wickey selected a few amber colored bottles containing herbs from those sitting on his desk, and after an unusual testing process, determined that he needed safflowers, golden seal, and black walnut to correct his problem.

He said he asked Doctor Wickey, "Can you tell all of that by just looking in my eyes?" Wickey nodded, he said, and told him the eyes are the window to the body, then he leafed through a book laying on his desk and pointed out several pictures of the eyes.

Wiley said Doctor Wickey showed him the title page featuring the picture of a man with "doctor" in front of his name to impress him with the fact doctors were using this method to diagnose.

Wiley said when he asked Doctor Wickey how much he should cut back on the Orinase, he was told to cut back gradually, then quit altogether, because the herbs he had prescribed would take care of the problem.

Doctor Wickey gave him a diet to follow, he said, along with the list of herbs to take, and instructed him to buy them from his son at the counter out front. Wiley said he bought the three herbs for $19.67, got a receipt, and left.

"No further questions, Your Honor," Michael Minglin said as he confidently strolled back to the prosecution table.

"Does the defense wish to cross examine this witness?" Judge Anderson asked.

"Yes, Your Honor," Jerrald Crowell replied.

Q. Sergeant Wiley, would an investigation of this nature normally be handled by The Indiana State Police instead of local law enforcement officials?

A. Yes. We are technically the investigative arm of the attorney general's office when they so request.

Q. Exactly what did they say you were to investigate?

A. The unlawful practice of medicine by Solomon Wickey.

Q. Did you go to the Wickey place alone?

A. No. Detective Dennis Guillaumes was in the surveillance unit.

Q. Exactly what was the purpose of having a surveillance unit?

A. Basically, he was to be there…just to be in the general vicinity.

Q. You stated that you wore a body transmitter. Did Detective Guillaumes monitor that transmitter?

A. Yes. In case something would occur.

Q. Do you always wear a transmitter during an investigation?

A. No. The body transmitter was more for, like, it's for my protection.

Q. Did you have reason to believe you would be in some sort of danger?

A. It's standard procedure in cases like this.

Q. And what kind of a case was this?

A. I understood drugs were possibly involved.

Q. This was a drug bust?

A. Potentially.

Q. Are such investigations usually recorded when the language is important to the investigation?

A. I can't say they never are. It's not my practice to record them.

Q. Did somebody tell you how you were to conduct the investigation?

A. I met with Michael Minglin and Janet Wiley and talked to them about the case.

Q. Did you talk to the Adams County Sheriff about Solomon Wickey?

A. No, I did not.

Q. Was your visit to Solomon Wickey solely for the purpose of entrapment? Yes or no?

A. Well, yes, you might say so.

Q. Did you see any kind of medical instruments or equipment in his office?

A. No, nothing like that.

Q. When you visited Solomon Wickey's shop did all of the people you saw coming and going have an appointment to see Wickey?

A. No. Some people came in to buy herbs and left without seeing him.

Q. How many people were in the waiting room when you were there?

A. Several. Ten or twelve. Could've been more.

Q. Did you notice any signs on the premises?

A. In the waiting room there were some signs having to do with herbs, newspaper articles, cut outs, things of that nature.

Q. Did you see any signs or posters signed by the sheriff of Adams County?

A. No, and I had looked for those too. I heard previously that Wickey had signs up saying that he was not able to prescribe medicine, or something like that. I looked for those. They were not there as far as I could see.

Q. Were there any signs on the outside of the building?

A. No.

Q. You didn't see any such signs? No signs bearing the Adams County Sheriff's signature, either inside or outside the building?

A. Right. There were none visible to me, and I was, like I said, looking for them. I didn't see any signs of any kind.

Q. You referred to Mr. Wickey as doctor?

A. Yes, that's correct.

Q. Did Solomon Wickey refer to himself as doctor?

A. No.

Q. At any time that day?

A. No.

Q. Did you hear anyone else on the premises call him doctor?

A. No.

Q. Why did you refer to him in that way?

A. I understood that's what I should call him.

Q. What medications did the gentleman from Terre Haute say Solomon Wickey told his wife not to take after her surgery?

A. He didn't specify. He just said medications. He didn't specify them by name.

Q. When they went into Mr. Wickey's office, could you hear their voices and their conversation clearly above the din of ten or twelve people sitting next to you in the waiting room?

A. Well, no, not real clear, but I heard someone, who I believe was Mr. Wickey, tell her she should take vitamins.

Q. Are you sure the voice belonged to Solomon Wickey?

A. No, I'm not absolutely sure.

Q. You testified that your story about having diabetes was made up. Is that correct?

A. Yes.

Q. Why did you choose diabetes as your invented problem?

A. It was suggested because there is no cure for diabetes.

Q. Who suggested diabetes to you?

A. It was discussed when I went down to the attorney general's office.

Q. Did you, in fact, have diabetes at the time you saw Solomon Wickey?

A. Not to my knowledge, no.

Q. Did you have high blood sugar at that time?

A. No, not to my knowledge.

Q. Did you check that out with a doctor?

A. Approximately a year before that I had a complete cardio physical at Krannert Institute in Indianapolis, and they said I was in perfect health.

Q. After looking into your eyes for only a few seconds, Solomon Wickey told you that you didn't have diabetes, but did have a slight heart problem. Is that correct?

A. That is correct.

Q. Did you do any checking since that time to find out whether you do have a slight heart condition?

A. No. To my knowledge, and reading the law, whether I actually had those diseases or not was not a determining factor in the violation.

Q. Sergeant Wiley, I have a copy of your medical records. Is this diagnosis that you have a slight heart murmur correct?

A. Well................

"No further questions, Your Honor."

Judge Anderson said, "Mr. Minglin, you may call your next witness."

In answer to Minglin's questions, the witness stated his name, Max E. Coburn, address, Ft. Wayne, Indiana, and he said for the past fifteen years he had been employed by the Indiana Attorney General's office as an investigator for the consumer protection division.

He told the court that Michael Minglin came to his office on the second floor of the Indiana State Capitol Building in Indianapolis, and asked him to go to Solomon Wickey's place of business northwest of Berne, Indiana, to notify him of the attorney general's intention to ask the Adams County Circuit Court to issue a restraining order to close his business to prevent him from unlawfully practicing medicine without a license.

Max Coburn described Solomon Wickey's herb shop; the building, cars in the driveway, people in the waiting room. Everything!

In detail, he told the court about two women who went into the back room office, and how he plainly heard Doctor Wickey say, "This is badly ulcerated." Almost immediately afterwards, he said, the two ladies came out and handed a piece of paper to the young lady behind the sales counter. Looking at the paper, he said, she yelled, "Dad, we don't have this!"

He went on to say, an Amish man, he assumed was Doctor Wickey, came out from the back room whistling as he walked through

114

the waiting room followed by the two women, and went outside to a stack of ten or fifteen boxes the UPS driver had just delivered. He tore into a box, Coburn said, and handed a package of medicine to one of the women.

"Did you speak directly to Solomon Wickey?" Minglin asked.

Max Coburn said yes he did, and when he addressed the man as Doctor Wickey, he responded. Coburn said he asked if he could see him for a minute in private. Wickey nodded and took him into the buggy shed. Coburn related that he said, "It is pretty evident from what I've heard today that it would be hard for you to deny that you are practicing medicine in there."

He said Wickey said, "I guess," or something like that.

"I have no further questions, Your Honor."

"Does the defense wish to cross examine?"

"Yes, we do, Your Honor," Jerrald Crowell answered.

Standing directly in front of the witness, Crowell said, "Mr. Coburn, why do you say, Doctor Wickey?"

A. I addressed him the way everybody else around there addressed him.

Q. Who, for example?

A. Nobody in particular.

Q. People who were waiting?

A. No.

Q. The young woman behind the counter?

A. No.

Q. Did you ever hear Mr. Wickey call himself doctor?

A. No.

Q. How many people were in the waiting room when you were there?

A. Several. Eight or ten.

Q. Were they talking to each other?

A. Yes.

Q. So it was sufficiently noisy in the waiting room?

A. Yes, it was somewhat noisy.

Q. Did you see any signs around the premises, sir?

A. Oh, there were nature-type signs. That's all.

Q. Any signs there about whether he could prescribe, or anything like that?

A. No.

Q. You didn't see anything in that regard?

A. He had honey for sale, a big sign on it. The most prominent sign I saw read, HONEY FOR SALE BY THE GALLON.

Q. You didn't see any signs to indicate he could not engage in the practice of medicine or anything to that effect?

A. No.

Q. You testified that you saw two females go to the back room. Is that right?

A. I did.

Q. How long were they back there?

A. About fifteen or twenty minutes.

Q. Could you hear their conversation above the noise?

A. I could hear Wickey very plainly talking, but the women's voices were muted.

Q. What did you hear Mr. Wickey say?

A. He said, "This is badly ulcerated."

Q. Do you know what he was referring to when he said, "This is badly ulcerated?"

A. No.

Q. But you couldn't hear the women talking?

A. No.

Q. How good is your hearing?

A. Not a hundred percent, but average.

Q. How old are you, Mr. Coburn?

A. 58.

Q. You said Mr. Wickey opened a box and handed one of the women a package of medicine. Is that correct?

A. Yes.

Q. How big was the package?

A. A very small package. And I can't even tell you whether it was a box or a bottle.

Q. Could you tell us the exact size of the package?

A. No, I wasn't paying that much attention.

R. Could it have been a big package?

A. Yes, it could have been a big package.

Q. What would be the biggest size you think it might have been?

A. The corrugated box he tore into was about 12x18x12 inches. If he gave her the whole box it wouldn't be larger than 12x18.

Q. Tell the court exactly what was in the package.

A. I don't know for sure what it contained.

Q. Did you ask Mr. Wickey?

A. No.

Q. Did you ask the ladies?

A. No.

Q. Could it have been plant fertilizer?

A. Yes, I suppose it could have been.

Q. What made you think he was practicing medicine?

A. I heard the man say something was ulcerated.

Q. Are you absolutely certain the voice you heard was that of Solomon Wickey?

A. No.

Q. How did you know he was referring to something on the body of one of the women?

A. I would assume if he was in the room with two women, it would probably refer to one of them, but no, I couldn't prove it beyond a doubt.

Q. Did you send a report of your visit to Michael Minglin?

A. Yes.

Q. Now, Mr. Coburn, even though you could not clearly hear the conversation between Mr. Wickey and the two women, and you actually had no knowledge, or proof, of what was in the package he handed them, in your report to Michael Minglin did you state that without a shadow of doubt, Mr. Wickey was practicing medicine?

Jerrald Crowell let a few seconds of silence drift past as the witness stared at the floor without speaking.

"Answer the question, Mr. Coburn. Yes or no?"

A. Yes, sir.

Q. How long have you held your present position with the consumer protection division of the Indiana Attorney General's office?

A. Fifteen years.

Q. How many times in the past fifteen years did you recommend an indictment based on unsubstantiated, flimsy evidence?

A. Never.

Q. Why did you do so in Mr. Wickey's case?

A. It was expected.

Q. Were you aware at that time that it was against the Amish religion to hire an attorney?

A. I'm from Ft. Wayne, so I'm very familiar with the Amish.

Q. You were aware, then, that they cannot hire an attorney?

The question hit a raw nerve. Michael Minglin jumped up and yelled, "I object! What is the point of the question?" he shouted at Jerrald Crowell. "Obviously, you and Mr. Harrison are representing him, and I assume you are being paid.

"I object to the question, Your Honor. It is irrelevant."

Crowell shot back, "I didn't say represent. I said hire."

"Objection overruled!" the judge declared.

"I have no further questions, Your Honor." Crowell said on his way back to the defense table.

"This court is in recess for lunch. This cause of action will be resumed promptly at 1:30." The rap of Judge Anderson's gavel resoundingly echoed off his solid oak desk.

When Michael Minglin stepped into the hallway outside the courtroom, several people observed a big, husky, blonde man who intentionally stepped in front of him, and pointing a threatening finger, declared in a powerful, commanding voice, "If you put that man in jail, I will shoot you. I served as a Green Beret with the United States Army Special Forces. Solomon Wickey saved my young daughter's life after the medical people screwed her up and left her to die. If you do anything to that man, anything at all, I guarantee you I will make good on my promise to shoot you!"

The blood drained from Minglin's face as he turned, and hurried away. He was not having a good day.

When court re-convened after lunch, Judge Anderson instructed Michael Minglin to call his next witness. Minglin called Dr. George Merkle to the witness stand. This witness had not been present in the courtroom that morning, had not heard testimony of other witnesses, nor was he aware of the audience reaction and participation being sanctioned by Judge Anderson.

Through Michael Minglin's questioning, Dr. Merkle presented credentials to qualify as the state's expert witness. He told the court that he was a thirty-eight year old physician practicing medicine in Bluffton, Wells County, Indiana. He attested that he had been licensed in the State of Indiana since 1970, was certified by the American Board of Family Practice, and had been president of the Wells County Board of Health for the past eight years.

Dr. Merkle told the court that the Wells County Board of Health received a complaint against Solomon Wickey from a citizen, and that he personally felt responsible for following up on that complaint. He said Dennis Zawodni, the Wells County Sanitarian, was assigned the task of investigating Doctor Wickey, and that he, in turn, brought the Indiana State Board of Health into the investigation.

Dr. Merkle said, as part of that investigation, he made an appointment to see Doctor Wickey at 9:45 A.M. on July 9, 1980.

"So, on July 9, 1980, you and Mr. Zawodni went over to see Mr. Wickey, is that correct?" Minglin asked.

"Yes."

"Dr. Merkle, could you tell the court what occurred on that occasion?"

Jerrald Crowell yelled, "I object, Your Honor! 1980 is in the wrong time frame."

Judge Anderson overruled Crowell's objection, saying he would make an exception this time, since Dr. Merkle was testifying as the prosecution's expert witness.

"As I was saying, Dr. Merkle, could you tell the court what occurred on that occasion?"

Dr. Merkle told the court that he had an appointment at 9:45 in the morning. He said he was accompanied by Dennis Zawodni. They entered what appeared to be converted milk barn on the north end of a large white barn out in the country, where a number of people were seated on metal folding chairs in a makeshift waiting room that had signs and statements on the walls stating clearly that medical practice was not allowed on the premises.

As soon as we entered the building, the young lady behind the counter asked if we had an appointment with Doctor Wickey?"

"Did she use the word doctor?" Minglin interrupted.

Yes. She said do you have an appointment with Doctor Wickey?" I told her yes, I had a 9:45 appointment. She asked the date of my last appointment, and I told her I was a new patient."

"If you will, please describe what you call his office."

Dr. Merkle told the court that this basically was a whitewashed room about 15x30 feet with a long counter at one end. Shelving stood against a wall behind the counter, but did not reach the ceiling. The shelves were lined with various packages and some bottles of what appeared to be herbs and natural foods. He said he and Dennis took a seat along side six other patients in the waiting room. After a lengthy wait, the young woman called his name, took him into the examining room, and introduced him to Doctor Wickey.

Dr. Merkle said he introduced himself as Doyle Guinn, and told Doctor Wickey he was visiting his niece in the Berne area and came to see him because of severe, crushing chest pain under his breast bone, spreading into his left shoulder, neck and arm. The pain, he said, was much worse after walking, bending, lifting, or any kind of exertion. He said he told Doctor Wickey that he worked as a watchman. He said he knew he was overweight, and lamented that he was afraid he was having a heart attack because he had nearly passed out earlier that morning.

He said Doctor Wickey asked him several questions about his family history, if anyone else in the family had had problems like this, and he told him that his father and brother had severe heart disease, and both had suffered heart attacks.

Doctor Wickey didn't comment on his symptoms, but, instead, picked up a small pen light and a thick lens from his table, and briefly looked in each of his eyes for about five seconds. Dennis Zawodni acted as scribe, to write down diseases as Doctor Wickey identified them, along with the recommended treatment for each.

The examination, which, he said, continued for some ten or fifteen minutes, consisted almost entirely of palpations with Doctor Wickey's open hand and his flexed index finger, particularly in one place on his back. At the end of the examination Doctor Wickey said, "That's what I thought. You don't have any heart problem. There is nothing wrong with your heart."

Dr. Merkle told the court he had rehearsed his act well, but in spite of the fact the history he presented was classic for unstable angina, Doctor Wickey told him he didn't have a heart problem, but said he did have gout and high uric acid.

He said Dennis Zawodni wrote down the problems as they were identified, which he considered to be a diagnosis. Doctor Wickey mentioned bile, and gall, and vascular, and for each diagnosis Mr. Zawodni wrote down the appropriate prescription; lecithin, and two products called HLBX and HYA. At that point Dr. Merkle said he asked Doctor Wickey if he should continue taking his insulin. He said Doctor Wickey seemed surprised, and said, "Oh, you have sugar?" Dr. Merkle answered, "Yes." Doctor Wickey said, "No, you don't!" and urged him to stop taking his regular insulin because, he said, "You don't have a sugar problem."

Dr. Merkle said Doctor Wickey told him to stop at the counter out front and his daughter would get the herbs for him. He and Dennis left the office.

Out front, he said, the young woman set five preparations on the counter and told him the price was $45.85. He picked up one of the bottles and while he was looking at it Doctor Wickey suddenly appeared behind the counter, giving him an opportunity to ask what he owed him for the office call. He replied, "You don't owe me anything. They won't let me charge."

Dr. Merkle said he asked, "Who won't let you charge?" and Doctor Wickey answered, "The sheriff. They have been here. They don't want me to help people, but you can buy herbs here."

Dr. Merkle said he thanked Doctor Wickey, and announced that he didn't have $45.85, so would not be purchasing the tablets and powders. He and Dennis left.

"It is apparent," he told the court, "that from what little direct and indirect experience I've had with Doctor Wickey, he is really attempting to practice medicine, and he's doing a very poor job of it. He is giving faulty advice and thereby endangering the lives of those he treats."

Dr. Merkle's prejudice against Solomon was glaring.

The audience went wild. Some booed him. A few men jumped to their feet, yelled obscenities and shook their fists at him. The majority, shocked by the malicious hogwash they had just heard, sat there shaking their heads in disbelief. Dr. Merkle squirmed in his chair on the witness stand. Glistening sweat pods gathered on his brow and soaked the hair at his temples before running down his cheeks to drip off heavy jowls onto his protruding belly.

Judge Anderson rapped for order. In an effort to cool sizzling emotions, he said, "We will take a ten minute recess."

After the recess, Michael Minglin turned to Jerrald Crowell and Andrew David Harrison, pursed his lips into a smirky little smile, and said, "Your witness, counselors."

Jerrald Crowell nodded his acknowledgement, but sat quietly studying the witness for several minutes before getting to his feet.

George Merkle was grossly overweight. His eyes looked like two glass beads lost in a puffy face dominated by fat lips, and cheeks that cascaded into one chin after another, tightly cinched by a buttoned, starched shirt collar and a necktie. His swollen hands extended into fingers resembling helium-filled balloons, while his bulging belly fell between separated thighs when he sat, and two obscenely strutted ankles spilled precariously over his shoe tops. To Jerrald Crowell, the witness mirrored the picture of a glutton who had lied obsessively on the witness stand.

Crowell, standing directly in front of the witness, launched into his cross examination.

Q. Dr. Merkle, please tell the court how you originally heard of Solomon Wickey.

A. The board of health...that's the Wells County Board of Health...had a complaint about him from a citizen.

Q. What was the nature of that complaint?

A. Doctor Wickey prescribed a variety of herbs for her grandson, and she didn't know what they were.

Q. How old was the child?

A. Four or five.

Q. Did the grandmother ask Mr. Wickey what each herb was for?

A. No.

Q. Why not?

A. She didn't take him to see Doctor Wickey.

Q. Who took the child to see him?

A. His mother.

Q. And Mr. Wickey explained the purpose of the herbs to the mother?

A. I suppose so.

Q. Was the grandmother the child's guardian?

A. No.

Q. Did the child live with the grandmother?

A. No.

Q. Did the grandmother complain to you, or to the board of health directly?

A. No, not directly.

Q. Then to whom did she complain?

A. She told one of the nurses, and the nurse told me.

Q. Do you know the grandmother?

A. Well, I know who she is.

Q. Please tell the court her full name.

Dr. Merkle was reluctant to answer the question. His face turned scarlet, while sweat dripped furiously off his chins. He finally croaked, "Lois Ellen Johnson."

Q. Where does Mrs. Johnson live?

A. In Poneto.

Q. Is Poneto in Wells County?

A. Yes.

Q. Did the child and his mother live in Wells County at that time?

A. No.

Q. Mr. Wickey lives in Adams County, does he not?

A. Yes, I believe so.

Q. Did you, or anyone at the Wells County Health Department, contact the Adams County Health Department about this complaint?

A. Yes, but they refused to take any action.

Q. What business was it of the Wells County Board of Health what went on in Adams County?

A. Well, people from Wells County went over there to see him.

Q. Do they not have a constitutional right to do that?

A. Yes, but it was not necessary. We have doctors in Wells County.

Q. Dr. Merkle, would you personally benefit financially if Mr. Wickey was found guilty of these charges and forced out of business?

A. I imagine all physicians in this general vicinity would benefit.

Q. Let's go back to Mrs. Johnson. Please tell this court how you know her.

There was no response from the witness.

Q. Dr. Merkle, is it true that Mrs. Johnson was employed at that time by the Wells County Board of Health as a secretary; your secretary?

A. Yes.

Q. Did she actually register an official complaint?

A. Well, she told us about it.

126

Q. Did the Wells County Board of Health receive a complaint from anyone other than you and your secretary?

A. Well, there were several people from Wells County going over there to see him.

Q. Did anyone other than you and your secretary complain about Mr. Wickey? Yes or no?

A. Dennis Zawodni sent a formal complaint to the State Board of Health.

Q. Did anyone not connected to the Wells County Board of Health complain about Mr. Wickey?

After a long silence, he swallowed hard and whispered, "Not to my knowledge."

Q. Dr. Merkle, you stated that you had an appointment to see Solomon Wickey at 9:45 on the morning of Wednesday, July 9, 1980. Is that correct?

A. Yes. Dennis Zawodni made the appointment for me under the name of Doyle Guinn.

Q. You also stated that the young woman working behind the counter asked if you had an appointment with Doctor Wickey. Is that correct?

A. Yes.

Q. Did she use the word doctor?

A. Yes. She asked if I'd had a previous appointment with Doctor Wickey, and I told her no, I was a new patient.

Q. Are you aware, sir, that Mr. Wickey did not take appointments, but saw people on a first come, first served basis only, prior to December, 1981?

A. No.

Q. Since he didn't see people by appointment when you went there in 1980, please tell this court how you became an exception.

A. Uh............

Q. Isn't it true, Dr. Merkle, that actually you did not have an appointment at all?

A. Well, I seemed to remember that Dennis made one for me.

Q. You made that up just to make Mr. Wickey look guilty of trying to imitate a medical doctor. Isn't that true?

A. I guess so.

Q. Now think hard, Dr. Merkle. Remember you are testifying under oath here. Did the young woman refer to Solomon Wickey as Doctor Wickey, or use the word doctor at all?

A. Well, perhaps I was mistaken.

Q. Doctor, do you know the meaning of the word perjury?

A. Yes.

The overburdened witness stand chair creaked and groaned mightily as Dr. Merkle shifted his weight from side to side. It was quite obvious that he was becoming increasingly irritated by Jerrald Crowell's questions.

Q. Will you tell the court the meaning of that word?

A. It means to swear falsely.

Q. Correct. Now let me restate the question. Did the young woman behind the counter refer to Solomon Wickey as Doctor Wickey, or use the word doctor at all?

A. No, he whispered.

Q. Did you, in fact, hear anyone in the room, or on the premises, refer to Mr. Wickey as Doctor Wickey?

A. No.

Q. Did you ever hear anyone, at any time, call him Doctor Wickey?

A. No, he squeaked.

"Speak up, Dr. Merkle," Judge Anderson ordered. "We cannot hear you."

A. No, he repeated, looking at the floor.

Q. Doctor, let's talk about the time you spent with Mr. Wickey. When you went in there and sat down in front of him, did he ask your name?

A. No, I introduced myself as Doyle Guinn.

Q. Did he fill out any kind of chart or paperwork using the name?

A. No.

Q. You also stated that you immediately launched into your well-rehearsed list of symptoms. Did he ask you for that information or write any of it down?

A. No.

Q. What did he do?

A. He looked in my eyes for a few seconds using a magnified glass and a small pocket light, and told me I didn't have a heart problem, but did have high uric acid.

Q. And he also said you didn't have sugar diabetes?

A. Yes.

Q. Did he ask you anything at all about your physical condition?

A. Well, no, not exactly.

Q. So you made up the entire story about him taking your family history and giving you a fifteen minute physical examination. Is that right?

Dr. Merkle was speechless. He was unwilling to admit that this entire senseless court action was based on nothing more than his own vindictive greed. Words just would not come.

Jerrald Crowell nodded his head at Andrew David Harrison as he walked back to the defense table and took a seat. Harrison immediately got to his feet to take over the cross examination of the witness.

Tall, handsome, red-headed and imposing, Harrison was much more dramatic in his courtroom presentation than Crowell. It was his habit to point his finger, to emphasize words in a derogatory, belittling way, and to lean on the witness stand, starring in the face of a witness he was trying to intimidate. Going after George Merkle was going to be a pleasure.

Q. Doctor, you mentioned there were signs about not practicing medicine on the premises. Could you be more specific? What did the signs say?

A. I do recall they were signed by the sheriff of Adams County, which kind of surprised me because Dennis had not told me anything about this before going out there, and as I recall, something was said in these notices to the effect that medicines cannot be prescribed on these premises under an order of the sheriff of Adams County. I'm sorry, I don't recall the exact wording, but that was the gist of the notices.

Q. And there was more than one notice?

A. Yes, there were several. I would say that there were three or four notices on each of three walls in the room. Two or three notices outside on the door as you went in. So there was adequate notification.

Q. Doctor, how good is your eyesight?

A. I have perfect eyesight.

Q. Now think carefully, and remember you are still under oath. Tell this court, did you see even one sign on those premises that mentioned medicine, or that was signed by the sheriff of Adams County?

After a long agonizing silence, he whispered, "Well, perhaps I was confused about that."

Q. Dr. Merkle, will you please describe the medical instruments and equipment you saw in Solomon Wickey's office?

A. There was none to describe.

Q. Did you see anything to resemble medical equipment or instruments?

A. No. He did have a heavy, homemade, wood table that resembled a chiropractic table, though.

Q. Anything else?

A. No.

Q. His only equipment, if you can call it that, was an iridology glass and a pen light. Is that correct?

A. Yes.

Q. Other than herbs, did you see any medical remedies or preparations in his office or on the premises?

A. No.

Q. Doctor, please tell the court how herbs benefit the human body.

A. They're useless.

Q. How do you know they're useless?

A. Well, because I don't know anything about them.

The audience broke into gales of hearty laughter at Dr. Merkle's arrogant, conceited opinion of his own importance.

Q. Doctor, tell me, do you heal people?

A. Yes, I heal people every day.

Q. You make the skin grow and heal wounds?

A. Yes! Yes, I do!

Q. What chemical formulas do you use to make skin grow?

A. Well, I'd have to look that up.

Q. Is it true that not you, nor any doctor, can made skin grow. Only God can heal wounds and make skin grow?

A. Yes, I suppose so. Actually, God plays a very important role in healing.

Q. When you went out to see Mr. Wickey, did you, in fact, have a heart problem?

A. No.

Q. Did you have diabetes?

A. No.

Q. Doctor, how would you describe your health?

A. I'm in perfect, robust health.

The absurdity of that statement brought howls of laughter from the audience. Even the judge joined in.

Once he had composed himself, attorney Harrison continued.

Q. If a patient in the same physical shape you're in walked into your office, what would you do?

A. I would be gravely concerned.

Q. Would you agree that a controlled diet would solve a lot of physical problems for people?

A. No.

Q. You don't think diet has anything to do with physical problems?

132

A. Certainly a judicious diet, exercise, and general principles of good health are applicable in a lot of diseases, but a good control of a diet without specific medical help is of little value in most cases. There is one thing you didn't ask me...if I had uric acid. I don't have high uric acid. I have gout.

Q. Does uric acid contribute to gout?

A. No.

Q. According to the medical dictionary, "When uric acid is present in urine, its salts are found in the joints, causing gout, and is sometimes the major cause of kidney stones, as well." Is that correct?

A. Yes.

Q. Doctor, it sounds like everything Mr. Wickey told you out there that day about your health was basically true, was it not?

A. Certainly. He is a very good diagnostician. He practices good medicine. That's what I had heard. Everybody told me he is a miracle doctor. They all think he is one of the best doctors in this area. That's pretty general knowledge, as a matter of fact, but he isn't a legal doctor.

Q. Did you file a report about your visit to Mr. Wickey?

A. Yes, with the Wells County Board of Health.

Q. Did you also file a report and complaint with the State Board of Health?

A. Yes, I did.

Q. What was your complaint based on at that time?

Seemingly forgetful of having just admitted the untruthfulness of his various accusations, Dr. Merkle responded by reciting his well-rehearsed story.

A. My feeling was that on the basis of Mr. Wickey taking my medical history, physical examination, and prescribing of herbs, that he was practicing medicine. There was a statement on the wall of the building, I mean there were about twenty statements all over the walls and door saying medical practice is not allowed on these premises, or something to that effect. And my feeling was, on the basis of what I encountered on that day, that he was practicing medicine, and he was doing a poor job of it. He was making some misleading statements.

Q. In what respect?

A. For one thing, his explanation as to how vascular and uric acid and gall were connected. Something like, as the bile builds up in the kidneys it backs up into the vascular canals, you end up with parasites in your blood. Statements like that have no basis in fact.

Q. At least no basis in your profession?

A. There are no scientific......

Q. There is no basis in your profession, doctor?

A. Being robust and healthy, I had a hard time justifying the fact that I was expected to believe I had parasites or high uric acid.

Q. Why did you wait a year to file that complaint with the state board of health?

A. Actually, I didn't. No one called for the report earlier. During the next year, however, I encountered some other people, and heard of other people, associated with Doctor

134

Wickey. I figured that probably it was just a matter of time until he wouldn't be practicing medicine any more and as this began coming up subsequently in our health department meetings, I decided it was time to file the complaint. In fact, to the original paper that I had written summarizing my visit there, I simply added some other thoughts in regards to these other people.

Q. When you filed your report and letter of complaint, did you know that an Amish man cannot defend himself, nor hire an attorney to defend him?

A. Well, I might have heard about it. I'm not sure.

Q. Who told you?

A. I have several Amish patients…...

Q. Isn't it true that you filed the complaint with the state board of health only after you learned that an Amish man cannot defend himself, nor hire an attorney to defend him?

A. Possibly. I don't remember.

Q. So you knowingly leveled false, unsubstantiated charges against a man who could not defend himself. Is that correct?

Doctor Merkle fell silent, refusing to answer.

Q. Is that correct, doctor?

A. Well, I only heard about it. I didn't know for sure.

Q. Doctor, please tell the court the name of the person who told you.

Dr. George Merkle dropped his head and gasped for air. Hot, glistening tears spilled from his eyes, and streamed down his ruddy cheeks in wild abandon for everyone to see.

Andrew David Harrison quickly consulted with Jerrald Crowell, then turned to the judge and said, "We have no further questions, Your Honor."

Judge Anderson excused the witness.

Dr. Merkle stumbled from the witness stand. He unsteadily made his way out of the courtroom, pained by a sudden rash of hives, blinded by tears streaming down his face; a broken man, destroyed by his own vengeful scheming.

Judge Anderson instructed Michael Minglin to call his next witness. Instead, Minglin chose to read into the court record the statement of Maureen Rasmussen, Keeper of Records, Health Professions Service Bureau, State of Indiana:

August 19, 1983

To Whom it may Concern;

I have searched the records of the Medical Licensing Board of Indiana and find that Solomon Wickey of Berne, Indiana, is not now, nor has he ever been duly licensed to practice medicine in the State of Indiana.

The statement was properly attested and notarized.

With that, Judge Anderson complemented the audience on their exemplary conduct, and announced that the court would be in recess until nine o'clock on Tuesday morning, December 13, at which time the state could call its next witness.

Even before the judge's gavel fell to end the session of court, Michael Minglin and his entourage were quickly whisked out of the courtroom by a side door under the protection of the Indiana State Police, as per his request, in case Big Fist or the Green Beret might be lurking nearby, but the spectators were in no hurry to leave. They lingered in the courtroom, in the hallway, and in the courthouse yard to discuss the events of the day, especially the bold discrepancies and conflicting testimony by the state's witnesses.

Radio and TV reporters scurried to meet deadlines for their respective early evening news broadcasts. The Associated Press picked up the story, and by the time the eleven o'clock news hit the airwaves that evening, the story about Solomon Wickey, a well-known Amish man being accused of practicing medicine without a license in the State of Indiana because he was a proficient iridologist and herbal nutritionist who sold natural herbs out of an office attached to his barn, not only had crisscrossed the United States, it had also circled the globe.

Note: Information in this chapter is based on the Adams Circuit Court C-83-224 documents, individual eyewitness accounts, defense attorney's notes, and local newspaper accounts of the trial.

T E N

During the next two weeks, Solomon received several hundred letters of support from all parts of the United States and Europe. People in Europe found it hard to believe that someone could be hauled into court for practicing iridology and selling herbs, both of which are essential for maintaining optimal health in their way of thinking.

In that same two week period Michael Minglin submitted a motion to the Adams County Circuit Court asking permission to change, and broaden, his original accusations against Solomon Wickey. He also asked the court to allow three additional witnesses to testify for the state regarding events that purportedly took place prior to re-numbering the Indiana Medical Practices statute.

Confident that his motion would be granted, Minglin took the liberty of writing the official order to amend his original pleading the way he wanted it to read, and submitted it to Judge Anderson for his signature. Judge Anderson refused to sign the amendment motion, but did agree to hear Minglin's oral argument in favor of his motion when the trial continued.

Competition for a seat in the courtroom was unusually keen among Solomon's supporters on December 13th. Each of them had been a frequent visitor to Solomon's herb shop, knew him, his habits, his routine, and was disgusted with the state's fairytale presentation. They were eager to hear the defense attorneys present their side of the case.

The standing-room-only crowd had taken their places by the time court re-convened at nine o'clock. As soon as the standing ovation for Solomon ended, Michael Minglin approached the bench to ask Judge Anderson for a decision on his motion to amend the original pleading against Solomon Wickey.

After hearing Minglin's lengthy oral argument in favor of his motion, Judge Anderson ruled against that motion, and also dismissed one of the state's charges against Solomon by saying: "(1) the state cannot amend its original complaint to include acts the state alleges occurred as far back as 1979 and 1980, thus 1983 is the only year in question in this case, and (2) the state's case presented two weeks ago by deputy Attorney General, Michael Minglin, did not prove its second allegation…that Solomon Wickey acted deceptively. Therefore, the consumer fraud charge will be dropped."

The audience signified their approval of those rulings by a hearty round of applause.

Having lost his ability to call additional witnesses, Minglin's case ended.

"The state rests, Your Honor."

"Mr. Crowell, Mr. Harrison, is the defense ready to proceed?" Judge Anderson inquired.

"Yes, Your Honor," Jerrald Crowell replied.

Crowell began by making a motion, asking the court for a judgment to drop all charges against the defendant. In his oral argument to back up the motion, he said:

"The Indiana Medical Practices Act specifically sets forth an exclusion concerning the unlawful, or unauthorized practice of medicine, and it also states that the act shall not apply to any member of any church practicing its religious tenets so long as he does not make a medical diagnosis, prescribe or administer drugs or medicines, perform surgical or physical operations, nor assume the title of, or hold himself out to be a physician.

"There has been no evidence by the state's witnesses that the defendant held himself out to be a doctor or gave any medical diagnosis. He couldn't have even if he wanted to.

"Neither did the defendant violate the Indiana Medical Practices Act by prescribing or administering drugs or medicines, or performing surgical or physical operations. Under the broad definition of the practice of medicine as argued by the state, even Jesus Christ would be condemned. The defendant, Solomon Wickey, is a nutritional counselor following God's direction; nothing more."

Judge Anderson ruled against Jerrald Crowell's request for a finding to drop all charges against the defendant. "The state has proved its case to an extent," he said, "and the defense must now present its evidence to the contrary."

Jerrald Crowell called Dr. Eugene Watkins as the first witness for the defense. To establish him as an expert witness, Crowell asked several pertinent personal questions. In reply, Dr. Watkins told the court he was a doctor of naturopathic medicine, a nutritional consultant, and resided in Southfield, Michigan. He said he had this degree and that degree from various colleges and universities, a doctorate in natural medicine, and was the author of several books on naturopathic medicine.

Dr. Watkins, a very personable fellow, was definitely a cut above the average witness Judge Anderson encountered in his Adams County courtroom. The judge was fascinated by Dr. Watkins, impressed by his credentials, and quickly approved him as an expert witness for the defense.

In reply to Jerrald Crowell's probing questions, Dr. Watkins told the court that he had known Solomon Wickey personally since 1976, and knew him to be an excellent nutritional consultant. "He is a man of deep, abiding conviction and would not do anything that is contradictory to his faith.

"Solomon Wickey is a living herbal hero. When he started working with herbs in 1976, it was not generally an acceptable thing to do, but herbs were definitely on the edge of people's consciousness. At that time some people equated the use of herbs to witchcraft, or some strange occult practice.

"I kept telling them that using herbs to enhance one's health is in the Bible...in the book of Genesis where the Creator says, *'I have given you the herbs for your medicine.'* He didn't say the offer expires after a certain date, or when a new disease comes along. Neither did He mention side effects, or say, void where prohibited. Instead, in His infinite wisdom, He gave mankind an open-end promise."

In answering another of Crowell's questions, Dr. Watkins said, "Conventional medicine has some serious limitations. It's all about suppressing symptoms, not correcting problems. A medical doctor studies symptoms through scientific tests, and on the basis of those tests he makes a diagnosis. A diagnosis would be the name of a disease. Whatever disease he comes up with, he treats.

"A nutritional consultant treats the cause, not the symptom. He tries to build better health by giving dietary suggestions, making an analysis of how a person is doing, and making suggestions about natural changes that could come about by different food choices or a different lifestyle."

Michael Minglin objected rather loudly, complaining that Dr. Watkins was not a licensed medical doctor in the State of Indiana, and therefore was not qualified to make those statements.

Judge Anderson overruled the objection. After the audience finished applauding the ruling, he directed Dr. Watkins to continue.

"A good practitioner like Solomon Wickey can do a lot with, say, twelve herbs, because there are not thirty thousand different diseases. Some experts say there are only twelve, not more than twenty, known diseases that exist altogether. If you come right down to it, it's usually a question of oxygenation, or cleansing, or nourishing, or getting the trauma out of the body and restoring the electrical disturbance. If you can clean the bowel, clean the blood, and clean the lymph glands, a person will be much more comfortable. A good practitioner can do an awful lot to restore health with a few herbs, or herbal combinations, provided they're good quality."

Dr. Watkins said he knew of several clinical studies done with herbs. However, he added, to the best of his knowledge iridology has never been accepted by anyone in the medical profession. At this point he recited several verses from the Bible, including, "The lamp of your body is your eye.*"

"The iris reveals malfunctions in the body, and a good nutritional practitioner has knowledge of herbs that will correct those malfunctions. Iris analysis is not a diagnosis. It is medically worthless, but nutritionally sound. When a person goes to a restaurant and looks at a menu, he is practicing nutrition. Each one of us does it every day to survive.

"The Roman Empire was said to be disease-free for three-hundred years," he continued, "because of the good dietary practices of the Romans who followed the naturalistic teachings of Hippocrates." Dr. Watkins smiled as he quipped that the first nutritional deception involved an apple.

After overruling another of Minglin's continuous objections, Judge Anderson invited Dr. Watkins to present a sample of his standard nutritional health lecture, one he had taken to many countries and colleges throughout the world.

Dr. Watkins showed more than one-hundred slides to those present in the darkened courtroom, which he narrated as he went along. He patiently explained the nutritional benefits of plants growing in the wild, as well as organically grown herbs and fruits, which, he said, in his opinion qualify as nutritional foods and cures for ailments ranging from headaches to intestinal disorders, and much more.

At the conclusion of his presentation, after the lights were turned on, Judge Anderson thanked Dr. Watkins for sharing the slides, along with his wealth of information about herbs, with the court.

Jerrald Crowell said, "Your Honor, we have no further questions for this witness at this time."

"Mr. Minglin, do you wish to cross-examine the witness?" the judge asked.

"No questions, Your Honor."

"Dr. Watkins, I have a question," Judge Anderson said. "Do you feel that Mr. Wickey made a diagnosis when he told Sergeant Wiley he did not have diabetes, but did have other problems?"

"No. This man approached Solomon with a lie on his lips," Watkins replied. "This is a special case. I think Solomon simply responded to his lie."

"Thank you, Dr. Watkins. This court is now in recess until 1:45 for lunch."

With that said, Judge Anderson rapped his gavel, got up, and left the courtroom.

*****

When the court re-convened after lunch, the audience stood, cheering, when Jerrald Crowell called Solomon Wickey to the witness stand to testify in his own behalf.

In answer to Crowell's questions, the soft spoken Solomon said he was not guilty of practicing medicine. He told the court that he did not pose as a doctor, nor promote himself as a doctor; medical, or otherwise, and had never maintained a medical office. He said he sat in his herb shop adjacent to his barn, and people came to him asking for help. "What we do is teach them to balance the whole body, physically, mentally, and spiritually."

He said he provides nutritional counseling, supported by nearly three-hundred Old and New Testament Scriptures. Following the teachings of Jesus Christ was the most important thing in his life, he said. "I practice the teachings of Jesus Christ by teaching others a better way of life."

To support that contention, Jerrald Crowell picked up a copy of the King James Bible from the defense table, and requested that it be submitted into evidence.

Judge Anderson would not accept the entire Holy Bible as evidence, but did agree to permit Crowell to read twenty-two passages of pertinent Scripture into the court record. He randomly selected verses from a long list prepared by several of Solomon's loyal supporters.

Continuing in a somewhat different direction, Crowell asked, "Mr. Wickey, even in the broadest sense, can herbs be classified as medication?"

A. No. Some medication comes directly from herbs, though.

Q. Do you diagnose?

A. No. The body tells me what's wrong. It shows me the nutritional deficiencies through the iris of the eye, and I suggest herbs that will take care of the problem.

Q. Does that sometimes require changing the diet?

A. Yes.

Q. When people come to you for help, do you ask their name?

A. No. God sends them. He knows who they are.

Q. Is it true that you have a special God-given gift for helping people find better health?

A. Yes.

Q. How long have you had that gift?

A. I was born with it.

Q. Do you believe that God gave you the gift for the purpose of helping others?

A. Yes.

"We have no further questions for this witness at this time, Your Honor." Crowell said.

"Mr. Minglin, do you wish to cross-examine?

"Yes, Your Honor."

Q. Mr. Wickey, did you tell Sergeant Wiley not to take insulin?

Solomon responded by saying he never tells anyone to go against their doctor's orders, but said he didn't remember Sergeant

Wiley, or the specific details of his visit. "I analyze the deficiencies," he said, "but I don't determine the disease the person has."

"No further questions, Your Honor."

"Well, Mr. Minglin, I have a couple of questions for Mr. Wickey," Judge Anderson said.

Q. Mr. Wickey, did you say that you don't make a profit on the herbs you sell?

A. That's right. There's no mark-up on what we sell in the shop, but I get a bonus at the end of the month.

Q. Do you have a retail license?

A. Yes.

Q. Do you pay Indiana sales taxes?

A. Yes.

Q. Did the sheriff post signs inside, or outside, your shop?

A. No.

Q. Has the sheriff ever been to your shop?

A. Well, a deputy was there once.

Q. What was the nature of his visit?

A. Too many people were parking their cars up and down the road near my house.

"Thank you Mr. Wickey. You many step down."

At Judge Anderson's cue after the applause for Solomon died down, Andrew David Harrison called the Reverend Frank Miesse as the last witness for the defense.

In answer to Harrison's questions, Reverend Miesse told the court he was a Baptist minister from Springfield, Ohio, and also a practicing herbalist. He said he met Solomon Wickey and they became friends when he taught an herb and iridology class in 1976 which Solomon attended.

Miesse said it was quite evident from the beginning that Solomon had been blessed by a very unique God-given talent for helping people.

Q. Reverend Miesse, will you explain to the court what an herbalist, or a nutritional counselor, does?

A. God, working through nature, has all of the answers. God designed the body to heal itself. We simply assist people in doing this.

Q. So, Reverend Miesse, is it your opinion that by helping people, Solomon is following God's word, and that his reputation as a nutritional counselor is based on a gift from God?

A. Yes, absolutely. That's right!

Q. Then the state *persecutor* here is actually attacking a gift from God?

A. Yes! Yes, he is! Believe me, there is no coincidence in God. When God tells someone to do something, they'd better do it!

Q. Reverend Miesse, if the state is successful in prohibiting Solomon Wickey from practicing nutritional consultation, what do you think would happen?

Frank Miesse, sitting tall, raised his hands toward heaven, and in his strongest, most practiced pulpit voice, bellowed, **IT WOULD BE A SIN!**

Even though he had other questions for this witness, nothing could add to, or supersede, this unexpected, highly dramatic ending to the trial, so Harrison wheeled around, raised his hand in a gesture of salute, and said, "No further questions, Your Honor."

The courtroom erupted into a wild frenzy as the audience jumped to their feet for the longest, most boisterous round of applause in the whole trial.

When the room finally quieted, Judge Anderson looked at Michael Minglin and asked, "Do you wish to cross-examine?"

"No questions, Your Honor."

"If there are no rebuttal witnesses from the state," Judge Anderson said, "we will hear the final arguments. Mr. Minglin, are you ready?"

"Yes, Your Honor."

Michael Minglin's closing argument was brief and to the point. As he paced back and forth in front of Judge Anderson and the defense attorneys, directing a well-used pointing finger toward each of them for emphasis, he shouted that deciding whether Solomon Wickey was guilty or not, required careful examination of two separate points. (1) The state had to prove that he had violated the medical practice statute, which two of the state's witnesses had shown, and (2) the state had to prove that he didn't have a medical license, which had also been proven.

Minglin said, "The state has proved that Wickey's actions were not part of his religious beliefs. Quite to the contrary, it is clear that the defendant has gone beyond the spiritual aspect into the medical. Sergeant Wiley's testimony, along with the testimony of other witnesses, made it crystal clear that Wickey was practicing medicine when he examined eyes to spot physical ailments, then prescribed herbs as a cure.

"Wickey does have a license to sell herbs, and he pays taxes on that business, but by not having a medical license he is violating the Indiana Medical Practices law and must be prevented from continuing that activity.

"**HE IS GUILTY!**" Minglin yelled, shaking his skinny, clenched fist at the judge. "Therefore, the state demands that the temporary restraining order against Solomon Wickey be made permanent to protect the citizens of this state, and that he suffers punishment to the full extent of the law."

Michael Minglin unbuttoned his suit jacket as he arrogantly strolled back to the prosecution table, confident that he had won the case.

Jerrald Crowell took a quieter, more respectful stance in presenting the final argument for the defense.

"Solomon Wickey is not guilty of practicing medicine.

"Wesbter's dictionary gives us the following definitions:

Diagnose:

    (1) To determine the identity of an illness by a medical examination.

    (2) To classify or determine on the basis of scientific examination.

Diagnosis:

    (1) The process of determining by examination, the nature and circumstances of a diseased condition.

    (2) A scientific determination.

"According to testimony by Dr. George Merkle, expert witness for the state, and also by Dr. Eugene Watkins, expert witness for the defense, the medical profession does not accept iridology as being scientific. In fact, the medical profession does not accept iridology as having any value, whatsoever. Therefore, according to these witnesses, iridology does not qualify as a scientific medical examination. They also testified that natural herbs do not qualify as medication, nor as prescription drugs.

"Solomon Wickey does not diagnose. He does not prescribe drugs or medication. According to testimony by the state's own expert witness, Solomon Wickey could not possibly be practicing medicine.

"Solomon Wickey only practices the gospel of Jesus Christ as he is guided to do. He simply sat in his barn out on his farm, and people came to him. There has been no proof that he held himself out to be a doctor, even though state witnesses made false accusations to that effect. Accusations they recanted under cross-examination, I might add.

"The only accurate evidence in this case was that Solomon Wickey had an herb shop for which he had a retail license, and for which he paid sales taxes.

"The state's prosecutor failed miserably to prove that Mr. Wickey violated Indiana's vague statute governing medical practice."

Crowell argued that the entire law, effective since July, 1982, is unusually vague, and is unconstitutional, because it does not clearly define *diagnose, diagnosis,* and other terms. He insisted that he would be guilty of violating this law himself if he said a friend looked as if he had the flu, should take two aspirin and go to bed.

"Solomon Wickey did not step beyond the law. His only guilt in this case, Your Honor, is practicing his religious beliefs according to the Old Order Amish interpretation of the Holy Bible.

"Practicing one's religious beliefs was judiciously set forth by the Indiana Legislature as an exclusion to the medical practice law, but they did not precisely define which particular religion's beliefs would be acceptable in the interpretation of this law. Instead, the law says **any** member of **any** church practicing its religious tenets so long as he does not make a medical diagnosis, prescribe or administer drugs or medicines, perform surgical or physical operations, nor assume the title of, or hold himself out to be, a physician.

151

"The Indiana Medical Practices Act does not provide explicit standards, thereby rendering this law unconstitutional. Vague laws trap the innocent. It is a basic principal of due process that an enactment is void for vagueness if its prohibitions are not clearly defined. Where a vague statute abuts upon sensitive areas of first amendment freedoms, it inhibits those freedoms.

"Solomon Wickey's first amendment rights have been violated. He was not at fault. He was simply an easy target for those persons engaged in chicanery to further their own selfish agendas.

"Therefore, we, the defense team, respectfully petition the court to drop all charges against Solomon Wickey in this action, and vacate the temporary restraining order against him.

"Thank you, Your Honor."

And true to form, the audience stood for their last round of head-nodding and thunderous, supportive applause.

Judge Anderson told attorneys for both sides they had until December 29, 1983, to file final information with the court, and announced that he would rule on the matter by mid-January.

He ended the session by commending the approximately three-hundred Wickey supporters who had packed the courtroom every day of the proceedings, telling them he appreciated their attendance, their attention, and their excellent conduct. He rapped his gavel, and said, "This cause of action is now adjourned."

The curtain went down. The show was over.

*****

While spectators took their time about leaving the courtroom and saying goodbye to both new and old friends, Judge Anderson met with Jerrald Crowell, Andrew David Harrison, Michael Minglin and Janet Wiley in his chambers with instructions to present some kind of a settlement agreement to him before December 29th.

He suggested the following:

(1) A consent decree agreed to, and signed by, both parties.

(2) A proposed decree in the event the consent decree cannot be agreed upon between the parties.

Judge Anderson looked over his bifocals at Andrew David Harrison, the proclaimed expert in this kind of law, and said, "Attorney Harrison, you know what to do. Right?"

"Yes, Your Honor, I know what to do!"

No matter how often a lie is shown to be false,
There will remain a percentage of people
Who believe it to be true.

ELEVEN

Once back in Michigan, Andrew David Harrison quickly set about the task of writing a consent decree that would be fair to Solomon without violating the Indiana Medical Practices Act.

Article One stated that the judgment would forbid Solomon Wickey from performing any of the acts set forth in the Indiana Medical Practices Act. Harrison followed the wording in the Indiana statute, which prohibited Solomon from holding himself out as a doctor, maintaining an office for examination or treatment of persons suffering from disease, attaching the designation of doctor, M.D., D.O., physician, or surgeon to his name, or doing anything that would induce others to believe he was engaged in the practice of medicine or osteopathic medicine.

Article Two stated that the following acts would **NOT** be in violation of the Medical Practices Act, therefore the defendant would be allowed to:

- Observe a person's physical characteristics.
- Gather background and nutritional data concerning the person.
- Make nutritional analysis.

- Provide appropriate information concerning the nutritional status of the person.
- Make dietary and lifestyle suggestions, which do not knowingly contradict the recommendations or treatment of the person's licensed physician.
- Maintain his present place of business.

Andrew David Harrison's carefully worded consent decree prohibited Solomon from doing things he had not been doing anyway, and permitted him to continue doing everything he had been doing, while strictly adhering to the Indiana Medical Practices Act as it was written. It was an excellent document; short, concise, and clearly defined.

Jerrald Crowell, who found it to be fair and impartial, forwarded a copy to Michael Minglin, confident that both he, and Judge Anderson, would accept it as written.

Crowell's expectations were much too lofty, however. Judge Anderson made it clear that Solomon would not be convicted of the charges against him when he ordered the attorneys from both sides to submit a mutually agreeable consent decree to the court. Even so, Michael Minglin took the position that he won the case, and therefore had the power to slant the wording of the consent decree against Solomon.

Minglin accepted Harrison's paragraphs in Article One, which stated specifically what Solomon *could not do* by quoting the Indiana statute verbatim, but he drastically changed each paragraph in Article Two regarding what Solomon *could do.* According to Minglin's version of the consent decree, Solomon would have been in contempt of court if he sat in his herb shop and took a deep breath, or exhaled, in the presence of another person.

Minglin's version of the consent decree would prohibit Solomon from touching another person, using an instrument or device of any kind, or looking into a person's eye by any means, whatsoever. He would be permitted to recommend a diet, or engage in nutritional counseling only so long as it was not for the treatment, correction, or prevention of any disease, ailment, or defect he had observed. In an ambiguous gesture of generosity, Minglin stated that Solomon *could* sell herbs, vitamins, and professionally published materials that pertained exclusively to diet and nutrition. In the last paragraph he insisted that Solomon would be responsible for paying the entire cost of the trial.

Michael Minglin fired a copy of his revised consent decree back to Jerrald Crowell prefaced by a cover letter which strongly suggested that he was solidly in control of the situation.

Jerrald Crowell called Judge Anderson to advise him of their deadlock. After a lengthy discussion about the attorneys' need to meet to hash out their disagreements, and about how their various schedules had been juggled to accommodate the upcoming holidays, the judge agreed to Crowell's request for an extension of time in which to file the consent decree with the court.

Judge Anderson issued a new order to the attorneys of both sides directing them to file a mutually agreeable consent decree with the Adams County Circuit Court no later than January 12, 1984.

Michael Minglin, determined to have his own way, refused to agree with Crowell and Harrison about much of anything, including a location for the meeting to resolve the conflict regarding the wording of an acceptable consent decree.

Minglin insisted the meeting be held in the office of the Indiana Attorney General at the Indiana Statehouse in Indianapolis. Crowell contended that his office in Ft. Wayne would be a more appropriate location since it was about half way between Indianapolis and Andrew David Harrison's office in a suburb of Detroit, Michigan. Minglin steadfastly rejected Crowell's proposal, as Crowell did his.

Days and weeks passed without resolving the issue. Finally on Monday, January 9, only three days before the deadline, all three attorneys agreed to meet at the Delaware County Courthouse in Muncie, Indiana, a neutral location between Indianapolis and Ft. Wayne.

Jerrald Crowell and Andrew David Harrison arrived at the Delaware County Courthouse promptly at nine o'clock on Wednesday morning, January 11. Michael Minglin, Janet Wiley, and their assistants arrived fashionably late. Making his opponents wait stroked Minglin's ego. After all, in his opinion, he was the man in charge here.

It was apparent from the first "good morning" that Minglin and Harrison were at war; each determined to be the victor. Both sides went at each other for the next two hours with little, if any, compromise. Neither would concede a single word, not even a comma, in their respectively authored consent decrees.

About eleven o'clock, Jerrald Crowell and Andrew David Harrison shifted gears. Their many years of litigation experience became evident when they kicked into a good guy-bad guy act. Crowell had patiently argued in favor of the defense team's wording, presented points of law to substantiate their position, and tried his darnedest to negotiate a compromise. Now it was the shrewd, redheaded, mean guy's turn.

Andrew David Harrison was a very savvy, exceptionally observant lawyer. As a partner in a large herb company, he was also acutely aware of human nutritional needs, along with possible reactions when those needs were not met. When he observed Michael

Minglin beginning to have a problem with low blood sugar, Harrison enthusiastically engaged him in a heated debate about using the words "a," or "it," or "as," which continued nonstop for more than two hours while Minglin's blood sugar headed for the cellar. The lower his energy dropped the more conciliatory, the more agreeable, he became.

While Harrison argued over trivialities, Crowell quietly removed most of Minglin's language and substituted language from Harrison's original consent decree to broaden the scope of Solomon's business, knowing full-well it was Minglin's intention to not only narrow Solomon's business, but to eliminate it altogether.

Crowell successfully added two additional paragraphs which greatly benefited Solomon, but did not appear in either of the previous versions of the consent decree. When he read each of the corrected paragraphs back, Minglin surprisingly approved them without further ado. With each approval the Delaware County court secretary quickly changed the corrected paragraphs in the document to reflect the new wording.

Shortly after they agreed on the final sentence, the secretary had the new consent decree ready for their signatures. Michael Minglin signed the document, took his copy, and he and his staff were out the door before the ink was dry.

It was not until after he had eaten a good meal that Michael Minglin realized he had lost the entire case. Not only did he *NOT* get a conviction, he signed a consent decree that contained Harrison's original wording legalizing everything Solomon Wickey had been doing before the temporary restraining order was issued. Solomon Wickey *WON* on every point.

While Michael Minglin dined and took stock of the agonizing embarrassment of the situation, Jerrald Crowell and Andrew David Harrison headed to Berne to share the good news with Solomon.

When they pulled into the driveway, they saw Solomon and some of his sons walking through a field south of the house. Before the car came to a full stop, Harrison, still wearing his best three-piece business suit and new black leather loafers, was on the ground running toward Solomon through eight or ten inches of new snow, waving his arms and yelling, **"WE WON! WE WON! YOU'RE BACK IN BUSINESS!"**

Grinning from ear to ear, Solomon took his lawyers to his office in the herb shop where he signed the consent decree and handed the original to Jerrald Crowell. Once it was framed, his copy would hang on the wall in his office for all to see.

During one of the court recesses, Solomon asked Crowell and Harrison what he could do for them after they won the case. Without a moment's hesitation, Andrew David Harrison said, "I want a buggy ride!" So, as soon as they'd rehashed the events of the day, and concluded their business, Solomon sent the two older boys to harness his prized Standardbred and hitch him to a new buggy.

The entire family stood outside in the snow to watch Solomon and the boys ceremoniously bundle Andrew David Harrison into a warm, snuggly blanket there on the buggy seat. As the buggy rolled out of the driveway with Jerry Wickey at the reins, Solomon shouted, "Be careful, son. That's my lawyer!"

It was an unforgettable ride. Tiny icicles, firmly attached to tree branches, weeds, and wire fences, glistened and sparkled in the thin, late afternoon sunshine. The Standardbred stretched his long slim front legs into a smooth, magnificent trot, eager for a five or six mile run. Harrison had the time of his life.

Jerry Wickey, taking the long way around, stopped at his sister's house on the way back to share the good news. Anna Mae Jr., Solomon's only married daughter at the time, flew out of the house to meet them as soon as they drove into her driveway. Harrison yelled, **"Your daddy just won! Your daddy just won! His shop's open for business!"**

Reminiscing later, Harrison said he would always treasure that special moment, seeing the expression on her beautiful young face from his perch on the buggy seat. It was, indeed, rich payment for all the work he put into Solomon's defense.

First thing the next morning, January 12, 1984, Jerrald Crowell personally hand delivered the signed consent decree to Judge Anderson to meet the court ordered deadline.

About the same time, a news release from the Indiana Attorney General's office was being hand delivered to all of the newspaper, radio, and television offices in Adams, Allen, Jay and Wells Counties.

The Decatur Daily Democrat carried the story on the front page of the afternoon edition on January 12, 1984:

WICKEY CASE IS SETTLED

The Solomon Wickey case in Adams County Circuit Court, which has drawn widespread public and media attention, has been settled out of court with a consent decree signed by all parties.

According to an announcement received today from the office of Indiana Attorney General Linley Pearson, Wickey "signed a consent decree with the attorney general's office that was approved by Adams Circuit Judge Robert S. Anderson today, in which Wickey agreed to stop conducting acts which legally can only be performed by a licensed professional."

The announcement further stated that Wickey, a route 1, Berne, resident, "diagnosed illnesses by looking into patient's eyes, advised people to stop taking medicine for illnesses, and sold herbs for various physical ailments, but will no longer diagnose and treat patients in that manner."

The attorney general's statement further said, "The court settlement means that Wickey will still be allowed to observe a person's physical characteristics, but only for the purpose of making nutritional suggestions, not for determining disease.

"Wickey will still be able to maintain his business of selling herbs, vitamins, and other natural substances as long as they are sold for nutritional purposes only."

The consent decree says Wickey may "make dietary, lifestyle, and nutritional suggestions and recommendations so long as suggestions and recommendations are limited to nutritional needs."

Three days of hearings in the case were held in 1983, and Judge Anderson is expected to issue a decision in February on whether or not to grant the state's request for a permanent restraining order against Wickey's alleged illegal practices.

The decree assessed no costs against the state or Wickey.

Author's Note: The court documents contain no mention, whatsoever, of a pending decision to be made in February, or of making a restraining order against Solomon Wickey permanent.

On Thursday, January 12, 1984, in Portland, *The Commercial Review* carried the following lead paragraphs in its front-page article:

SETTLEMENT ANNOUNCED IN WICKEY CASE

An Adams County Amish man who sold herbs for physical ailments and diagnosed illnesses by looking into patients eyes signed a consent decree today agreeing to stop diagnosing and treating "patients," Attorney General Linley Pearson said.

"Solomon Wickey of rural Berne agreed to stop conducting acts which can only be performed by a licensed medical professional," Pearson said.

Local radio and television news broadcasters read the attorney general's announcement exactly as the news release was written without investigating the truth of the statements. The Associated Press likewise circulated the announcement as truth. After all, why doubt the validity of a statement from the Indiana Attorney General?

The next day, on January 13, 1984, *The Decatur Daily Democrat* ran a rebuttal to the attorney general's announcement condemning Solomon, not on the front page, of course, but on a back inside page along side the weather report.

WICKEY BACK TO BUSINESS AS USUAL

At least two members of the local legal system stated this morning that they believe Thursday's front page story in the Daily Democrat on the settlement of the Solomon Wickey case gave the wrong impression because a news release from the Indiana Attorney General's office, which was used in the story, was a misleading announcement.

The two men, who asked to remain anonymous, said today that the statement issued by Attorney General Linley Pearson was purely political in intent and attempted to hide the fact that the consent decree to which all parties in the civil suit agreed, allows Wickey to do everything he was doing before the suit was brought.

In fact, as a Fort Wayne Journal-Gazette reporter noted in today's edition, after visiting the Wickey home on route 1, Berne, "Wickey said he will formally resume analyzing client's nutritional needs by studying their eyes...a method called iridology...when he opens for business today."

The news release from Pearson's office, hand delivered in the region Thursday to many newspapers, television stations, and radio stations...stated that although Wickey "diagnosed illnesses by looking into patients' eyes, advised people to stop taking medicine for illnesses, and sold herbs for various physical ailments, he will no longer diagnose and treat patients in that manner."

According to the two local legal leaders, the consent decree includes several paragraphs, which allows Wickey to operate as he did in the past," they said. "He is free to operate exactly as he has done for a decade or more."

In an interview Thursday, Adams County Circuit Court Judge, Robert Anderson, said, "I'd say right now, he is back in business!"

"It's practically the same thing we were doing before," Wickey told a reporter about the decree, as he framed a copy to hang on his office wall. "I don't ask people to come, but if someone is in need, I want to do what I can to help. I feel that's part of my calling in life."

Other area newspapers, radio and television stations, ignored the local attorney's rebuttal in the Wickey case by choosing to allow the attorney general's news release to stand unchallenged. Thus, the general public in Adams, Allen, Jay and Wells Counties thought Solomon Wickey had been found guilty; especially folks in, and around, Berne.

Since Solomon forgives according to God's law, he simply filed his accuser's most recent attempt to persecute him under, **Give Them Enough Rope……**

Not surprisingly, careers and reputations were ruined as a result of this court action. The reputation Michael Minglin earned for himself was not at all what he intended. Dr. George Merkle lost his clinic, his credibility, and his position on the Wells County Board of Health. Dennis Zawodni moved on, and the Preacher was transferred to another church district.

On a happier note, in addition to his law practice, Andrew David Harrison started his own herb company, Good Herbs, Inc. in Troy, Michigan. Jerrald Crowell continued to enjoy a successful law practice until his death in May, 1997. Dr. Eugene Watkins' PURE HERBS, LTD. grew into a business of national prominence. God placed Solomon Wickey's feet firmly on an exciting new path of adventure and discovery.

"Be not deceived:
God is not mocked; for whatsoever a man soweth,
that shall he also reap."
Galatians 6:7

TWELVE

The notoriety surrounding the trial through media coverage and word of mouth served as a huge advertisement for Solomon and his work.

With each passing day the Wickey's driveway looked more and more like a crowded parking lot instead of a country barnyard. People came from everywhere. Friends and customers dropped by to congratulate Solomon, shake his hand, and welcome him back to work. Hundreds came gratefully. Many, some of whom were very ill, some diagnosed as terminal, had been fervently praying while they waited weeks, or months, for his help. They were grateful that with the blessing of Judge Anderson, the door to Solomon's herb shop was once again open to the public.

The Troublemakers, on the other hand, were enraged by the turn of events. Solomon had become much too friendly with English folks they complained among themselves. After all, it had been the English who filled the courtroom everyday, as well as English lawyers and witnesses who kept him out of prison and tried to make everyone believe the nonsense about him having some kind of a special gift from God.

Amidst a new volley of dirty tricks instigated by the Troublemakers, Solomon went on with his work, stayed to himself as much as possible, and in his prayers expressed his solemn gratitude for having been chosen for the opportunity to be in God's service to mankind.

In his opinion, it would be a sin not to use the talents God gave him regardless of the obstacles placed in his path. "If you want salvation," he said, "you can't bury your talents. You have to use them, and multiply them, no matter what people do to discourage you. Jesus clearly said so when He spoke about the gift of talents in both the Book of Luke, and the Book of Matthew."

In spite of the overwhelming challenges he faced in 1983, Solomon earned the distinction of being the top distributor of Nature's Sunshine products in the United States that year. In honor of the accomplishment the company invited him to their national sales convention, but it was against his religious beliefs to attend meetings where pictures would be taken and awards handed out, so he declined.

Folks in the home office, however, were especially eager to meet Solomon, to put a face with his name. The name of Solomon Wickey was known, and revered, not only by company officials, but also by every Nature's Sunshine distributor throughout the United States. They wanted nothing more than to talk to this mysterious legend in person.

Eugene Hughes, owner of the company, and Dale Lee, his national sales manager, put their heads together and decided to invite Solomon to be guest speaker at a manager's meeting scheduled for the last week of June, 1984, at the home office in Spanish Fork, Utah.

Dale Lee called Solomon's friend, Wendell Whitman, a relatively new Nature's Sunshine distributor in Warsaw, Indiana, to ask if he and his wife, Marilyn, would drive Solomon and Anna Mae to Utah for the meeting, and an extended two week vacation if Solomon accepted their invitation. Wendell quickly agreed.

As usual, Solomon was excited to be traveling. He and Anna Mae were ready and waiting when Wendell and Marilyn came to pick them up. Less than two hours later, they were on Interstate 80 in northern Indiana joyfully heading west toward Salt Lake City.

Solomon had a wonderful time. He sat like a king in the front passenger seat of Wendell's new Cadillac with a clear view of traffic, farm crops, and the entire country side. As they whizzed around slower moving traffic, Solomon saluted each driver with a big smile and a wave of his hand. Most drivers honked their horns and gave him a thumbs-up. After all, it was not every day they saw an Amish man wearing sunglasses fly down the highway in a shiny new Cadillac.

Solomon found crossing the Mississippi River near Davenport, Iowa where it runs almost three miles wide, to be an incredible experience. As they approached the broad, flat Mississippi River Valley lush with seemingly unending fields of corn and soybeans, Wendell handed him a pair of binoculars to play with. Once they were properly adjusted, Solomon read off the name of every boat and barge on the river, and used them to entertain himself as they sped across Iowa and Nebraska. He reported to his fellow travelers, in detail, the activities of every wild critter he spotted. The mountains of Colorado and Utah were particularly exciting. Through the binoculars he discovered aspen, ponderosa pine, majestic rock formations, rushing mountain streams, mountain bluebirds, mule deer, yellow-bellied marmot, golden and American bald eagles, mountain lion, and many other animals familiar to him only through pictures in a book.

The ladies in the backseat seemed to be full of conversation, private jokes and laughter as the hours and miles ticked away. Anna Mae and Marilyn, like two inquisitive young schoolgirls, dashed off to stretch their legs and explore at every stop along the way. Anna Mae was a wonderful teacher. She shared a wealth of knowledge with Marilyn by pointing out unusual wild flowers and various herbs by name. Then, of course, as they traveled beyond the Mississippi River they found regional plants they couldn't readily identify. The more they didn't know, the more they wanted to know about the land they were passing through.

When they arrived in Spanish Fork, Eugene Hughes was on hand to welcome Solomon and personally show him, Anna Mae, Wendell and Marilyn around the corporate offices. Dale Lee and his sales staff had planned an itinerary that would allow as many people as possible to meet and visit with Solomon during the next few days, including managers and supervisors in both the manufacturing plant and the sales department who were acquainted with his personal accomplishments, as well as his many contributions to the company.

Solomon joined Nature's Sunshine when it was a fledgling young company dedicated to making a difference in people's lives, even though at that time they manufactured and distributed only a handful of unusually high quality essential herbs. He was instrumental in ushering in a new era where people would take control of their own health care; an era that promised freedom from the addiction of prescription drugs and their debilitating side effects. He was also responsible for many of the herbal combinations the company added to their product line, both in the early days, and since. Without doubt, Solomon Wickey was a major contributor to the success and growth of this company.

The sales staff celebrated **Solomon's Day.** They pinned a large button with his name splashed across it onto his jacket. They took him on a private tour of the manufacturing plant which particularly impressed him because, as he said, "It was spotless! Clean enough to eat off the floor."

The sales department hosted a luncheon in Solomon's honor. For several hours he stood in a reception line so each employee could meet him, shake his hand, and share jokes or personal comments. Wendell appreciated being there with Solomon, while Anna Mae and Marilyn spent an enjoyable day with Dale Lee's daughter. She took them sightseeing in and around Salt Lake City, and to lunch at a lovely little tearoom. They spent the entire afternoon wandering around an ethnic street festival filled with music and dancers clad in bright, colorful costumes; the perfect place to shop, and indulge in huge mounds of sumptuous ice cream, which was considered a staple in the diet there.

Doug Clower, who had been chosen to host a tour of southern Utah on behalf of the sales department, put Solomon, Anna Mae, Wendell, Marilyn, and his wife, Judy, into a large luxury motor home early the next morning to begin the first leg of a truly great adventure.

It was an incredibly beautiful day for the two hundred-fifty mile drive down Interstate 15 between Spanish Fork and Zion National Park. Solomon was impressed by the scenery from the front passenger seat beside Doug. He laughed all the way, cracking one joke after another, but Doug remembered Solomon's big, rolling belly laugh as actually being more humorous than the jokes he told.

They arrived at Zion after dark, just in time for a late dinner at the Park Lodge, which featured venison, along with a bountiful spread of other favorite regional foods. The Wickeys and the Whitmans checked into small, individual cabins for the night, while the Clowers stayed in the motor home.

When the Clower's guests got up the next morning and stepped outside, their mouths flew open and their chins, long whiskers and all, practically hit the ground when, at an elevation of 7795 feet, they looked straight up at huge, towering red and white sandstone cliffs rising thousands of feet out of the canyon floor surrounding them. They were looking directly at one of the park's most famous geologic rock formations, The Three Patriarchs, named by a nineteenth century Methodist minister who settled in Zion Canyon. He was certain the three formations had been standing there in stately silence since long before man inhabited the earth.

The awesomeness of the sight, along with the energizing pure mountain air, prompted a before breakfast hike. The hiking trail took them past plunging waterfalls to a plateau filled with mountain flowers and herbs native to the area, most of which, according to folk lore, were used as medicines by Native American tribes, now extinct, or long since moved to distant reservations.

Back in the motor home after breakfast and a scenic drive through Zion National Park, they climbed out of the canyon along highway switchbacks hugging the canyon walls, to a channel cut through the sandstone cliffs known simply as *the long tunnel.* As they passed through a section of the tunnel where sandstone had broken loose, a brief glimpse of blinding sunshine slid down in a thin shaft to startle them. A few seconds later just as they started out of the tunnel, the huge downpour of a sudden rainstorm passed over, cascading an incredible amount of water over those red and white sandstone cliffs on its way to a canyon. What a fascinating experience for Indiana flatlanders!

Leaving Zion National Park on their way to an entirely different environment along the spectacular north rim of the Grand Canyon in northern Arizona, canyons became plateaus and red sandstone turned to ochre, seemingly by the swish of a Divine paintbrush.

The huge hole in the ground called the Grand Canyon was just too big for these midwesterners to comprehend. In silence, they walked along the rim of the canyon 9000 feet above sea level marveling at the geological rupture in the earth's surface, which ran more than one mile straight down to meet the Colorado River. Changing cloud patterns drifting in an azure blue sky highlighted various formations of the towering white and pink cliffs in the distance, making the scene new with every passing moment.

Sitting on the ground, they lingered to watch as the huge red-orange disc of the setting sun set the heavens ablaze as it slowly trailed off into the western sky, leaving a whole spectrum of color erupting like an angry volcano.

On the road again the next morning, they headed north toward Utah's Bryce Canyon National Park, traveling on a narrow, winding road through the Kiabab National Forest. The road was flanked on either side by dense conifer trees; pine, fir and spruce. When one of the ladies mentioned that the mountain side looked like it was covered with millions of Christmas trees, instead of responding to the comment with one of his usual quips, Solomon broke into a lively rendition of Jingle Bells. Everyone quickly joined in. They all laughed about singing a Christmas song on a hot day in early July, but by the time they were back in Utah, they had sung every Christmas carol they knew at least once; some, several times.

Bryce Canyon National park was like walking into another world, a fairyland created by sunshine playing tricks with the eroded red and white sandstone. The spirit of the people of the past remains very strong in this place that the ancient ones called the bosom of Mother Earth. These unmistakable, silent energies cling to every tree, to every rock, fill every drop of water, every particle of air one breathes; are all encompassing.

Doug stopped at a roadside canyon overlook where breathtaking views of red sandstone cliffs of porous rock rose thousands of feet in every direction as far as the eye could see. Geologically, Bryce Canyon is not a canyon at all, but a collection of amphitheaters carved millions of years ago by wind and water to create scenery whose indescribable beauty both abounds, and astounds. When they turned a corner on the other side of the park, the topography abruptly changed to coral sand dunes in the high desert, where little whirlwinds of sand playfully danced and cavorted, each to its own rhythm.

It was hard to leave such an enchanting place. In addition to scenery that fed the very soul, they found the rustic lodge at Bryce National Park comfortable and relaxing, the food good. But, alas, it was time to go.

As part of his scenic tour, Doug drove through Utah's Bad Lands, climbed 10,000 feet to cross Boulder Mountain, and stopped to let his guests explore an Anasazi Indian village where people lived and thrived in this high, arid desert for centuries before they mysteriously disappeared more than eight-hundred years ago.

At the north end of Lake Powell, Doug pulled into the Bullfrog Visitor's Center in the Glen Canyon National Recreational Area to check weather and lake conditions. He planned to rent a boat and take Solomon and his friends fishing early the next morning.

A park ranger lecturing there explained that Lake Powell was formed by the confluence of the Green and the San Juan Rivers with the Colorado River, making it the second largest reservoir in North America with 1960 miles of shoreline, more than the entire Pacific coast of the United States. He said that hundreds of side canyons, slot canyons, inlets and coves sheltering Indian ruins and other natural wonders, make Lake Powell a paradise for fishing, particularly for crappie, walleye, largemouth, smallmouth and striped bass. Mountain fishing. Solomon could hardly wait!

Doug Clower checked his guests into quarters at the Bullfrog Marina Inn, then, realizing that Solomon could not wait until the next morning to go fishing, hurried off to rent a boat.

"Captain Doug" expertly pulled an eighteen-foot bass fishing boat alongside the marina's dock. Solomon, Anna Mae, Wendell, Marilyn and Judy quickly climbed aboard, and away they went, skimming across shimmering, crystal clear blue water more than three-hundred feet deep in places.

Solomon had a fine string of huge striped bass to show when they got back to the marina. Could've had more, he said if he hadn't taken time out to put bait on Anna Mae's hook….a typical fisherman's story.

Anna Mae wanted a picture of Solomon with his string of fish. Knowing the Amish don't permit their pictures to be taken, Doug asked, "Well, how am I going to do this?"

"It'll be alright," she insisted. "Just as long as you only get his arm in the picture, it'll be OK."

To be on the safe side, as Bob Black had done many times, Wendell and Doug asked Solomon to turn his back to the camera while they both obliged by taking several pictures, being careful to aim the lens at the extended arm holding the string of huge striped bass. According to Solomon, the fun was mostly in the catching, but with no means to fry them, he handed the string of fish to a local fisherman for his pan. Lake Powell, and fishing there, were among the most memorable highlights of his entire trip.

The next morning, Solomon persuaded Doug to take the boat out on the lake again, not necessarily to fish, he said, but just to look around. Anna Mae and Judy went along, while Wendell and Marilyn chose to hang around the marina.

Doug headed for the Green Cathedral, a special place he'd discovered on a previous trip. He skillfully steered the boat through a very narrow slot canyon that suddenly opened into a little cavern that was no more than seventy yards across. Huge red sandstone ledges jutting out like wide, graduated stepping stones, were draped with garlands of green, drippy moss fed by natural sandstone seeps.

As they approached the cavern, Doug cut the motor. The boat silently drifted into this awe-inspiring little cathedral permeated with a Divine presence. The reverence of the place, the incredible bright blue sky forming a canopy above a circle of towering red cliffs, along with the smooth blue green water of the Colorado River, took Solomon's breath away.

Without a word, he reached for Anna Mae's hand, and together they stood facing the back of the boat where, in unison, they lifted their voices to God by yodeling in harmony in the Swiss German tradition of their ancestors. Echoes of the crisp, clear tones of their voices circling, bouncing and reverberating off the solid sandstone walls of the tiny cathedral raised the hair on the back of Doug's neck…an incredibly sacred spiritual experience he vowed he and Judy would vividly remember for the rest of their lives.

In fact, this trip with Solomon stood out among the many tours Doug Clower hosted on behalf of Nature's Sunshine. He was duly impressed with Solomon Wickey, with the precious simplicity of the man, and with his beliefs, his faith, his integrity.

The two men established a lasting, mutual friendship during the hours and days they sat side by side in the comfortable contoured seats up front in the motor home. Doug found Solomon to be very intelligent; equally as conversant on politics and world affairs as on herbs and health. He distinctly remembered lengthy conversations covering every subject imaginable.

For example, when the subject of the National Health Federation came up, Solomon related a story to Doug about a man back home, a member of the National Health Federation, who had followed every detail of his trial with great interest. After the trial, he insisted that Solomon meet privately with someone of authority in the National Health Federation to share ideas.

Solomon made it clear to anyone who would listen, that he wholeheartedly supported the philosophy of the National Health Federation, or any other organization that would strongly recommend political activity, as he did, particularly a concerted effort to lobby the United States Congress to pass laws to insure freedom of choice in all matters of personal health, without compromising more traditional methods.

(The National Health Federation, based in Monrovia, California, is a strong, broad based consumer health-protection organization dedicated to individual choice).

Solomon was very pleased when, a short time later, The National Health Federation hired a new lobbyist, and through his efforts on behalf of individual choice, they commanded a much stronger presence in the United States Congress.

Thanks to Doug and Judy Clower, Solomon's special vacation had been an exciting, fulfilling experience. Solomon and Anna Mae would forever be bound to Wendell and Marilyn, and Doug and Judy through the everlasting bond of memory.

As they left Spanish Fork on their way home, Wendell pulled one last trick out of a bag labeled "special memories." He had long known of Solomon's fascination with the huge commercial airplanes flying over Adams County farmland, and his curiosity about what they looked like inside.

Wendell stopped at the Salt Lake City International Airport where he arranged for Solomon to board a 737 Jet as it sat empty on the tarmac. An airline pilot volunteered to show Solomon through the plane. He let Solomon sit in the well-used captain's seat in the cockpit, while he pointed out the various instruments, and briefly explained how they work. As they slowly walked the entire length of the one-hundred-fifty passenger cabin, Solomon was invited to sit in a wide first class window seat...the perfect place to imagine the roar of the jet engines racing down the runway just before take off, how it would feel to lift off and, with his nose firmly pressed against the glass, watch the ground disappear beneath him as white, puffy clouds lazily drifted past the tiny window.

Solomon was jolted back into the reality of the moment when the pilot beckoned him to a seat situated over the wing for a look at the massive jet engines. He also pointed out the forward and rear galleys where food and drink is stored, and secured, during take-off and landing, and he opened the narrow door so Solomon could peek into the tiny lavatory in the plane's tail section. It was, indeed, the grand finale to a most incredible trip.

*****

Just ahead of the arrival of the fall equinox that year, Solomon's exceptionally keen insights reached an even higher plateau. Surprisingly, he found himself knowing the location and extent of a person's physical ills as soon as he or she entered his office, even before they sat down, or a word passed between them.

Invariably, a quick look through the iridology glass confirmed that insight. Call it instinct. Call it a hunch. Call it a natural talent. By whatever name, it was real. It worked. Keen insights were nothing new to Solomon. They had served as a dependable source of information since he was a small child. But this was different. Something new was happening.

For example, one day a man came into his office saying he'd been diagnosed as having lymes disease, and asked Solomon to help him. Before Solomon picked up the iridology glass to check the validity of the diagnosis, he became aware of a very different, unusual thought current regarding all aspects of the man's health, followed by explicit, unfamiliar instructions, which he later referred to a as a **release**, for lack of a better term. God seemed to be saying that in this particular instance the release would permanently correct the man's problem.

Solomon, who never questions God's wisdom, silently followed the instructions to the letter, and when he tested again there was no sign of the disease remaining in the man's body. That which had definitely been there only a couple of minutes before had suddenly disappeared. Every trace of it was gone. It was a startling experience that sent Solomon's brain spinning, with excitement and a million questions.

Solomon wholeheartedly believed that Jesus taught by example. Many are the stories in the Holy Bible about how He instantly healed the multitudes of sick and afflicted who sought His help, and said, "These things I do ye shall do also, and even greater things." Could it be possible that God was trying to reveal one of the

179

methods Jesus used to heal people? If so, had He chosen Solomon Wickey, another carpenter, as His modern day way-shower? It was all so puzzling.

From day to day a very humble Solomon went about the business at hand as he pondered the strange new instructions that seemingly removed all traces of the lymes disease from the man's body instantly, but he dared not confide a word of the experience to another living soul, lest they not understand, or question his sanity.

A few weeks later when another man came to him saying he had recently been diagnosed as having lymes disease, Solomon wasted no time in following his previous instructions to activate the mysterious release. As before, when he tested two or three minutes later, no sign of the disease remained in the man's body. Therefore, Solomon concluded that apparently the release instruction would remove lymes disease from any human body. It was definitely an interesting, thought provoking concept that would interfere with his sleep for many nights to come.

His fascination with this new discovery would have to wait. Another more important priority demanded Solomon's immediate attention. Now that the fall harvest was behind them, the Troublemakers had plenty of time to launch a vigorous new dirty tricks campaign against Solomon and his family.

No! No! No! Enough was enough!

It was time for Solomon and Anna Mae to move away from these abusive, mean spirited people.

For it is not ye that speak, but the Spirit of your
Father which speaketh in you.
Mathew 10:20

THIRTEEN

Solomon's newly constructed herb shop opened for business before the first daffodil burst through a lingering crust of snow in the spring of 1985, soon after he and Anna Mae settled into their new home across the driveway where there was plenty of room for a growing family to spread out in the big yard surrounding the two story house with twelve large rooms, beautiful solid hardwood floors, and an enormous kitchen.

Solomon bought 120 acres; 40 acres laying on the west side, 80 acres laying on the east side of county road 150E in Wabash Township southeast of Berne in the same church district where Dan and Lizzie Schwartz lived. With the exception of a stand of mature trees along the western property line, the entire farm was rich, flat production land.

The barn, huge even by Amish standards, stood towering above the house and the herb shop on the east side of the gravel road. Through his office window Solomon had a clear view of the house and the barn, as well as the yard and driveway in between.

If the Wickey boys were looking for work they would most certainly find it here. Solomon intentionally did little of the hard work himself. Instead, he acted as project engineer, teaching and overseeing his sons as they busied themselves that spring building fences and sowing alfalfa seed to turn about ninety-five acres into pasture and hay fields to feed their growing dairy herd, the draft horses, and the increasing Standardbred population. The remaining acres were plowed, disk-harrowed, and planted in corn and oats, which at harvest, would be stored at Lehman's Feed Mill in Berne to be ground into a supplemental ration of balanced nutrition for the animals and chickens, as needed. It was an exciting time for the Wickey family.

People from all walks of life found their way to Solomon's new herb shop as the public's interest in him and his work soared. They seemed to be drawn to the place through the humility and grace of this modest, mild-dispositioned man with the twinkling blue eyes and dark Amish beard. The quiet peacefulness they found there at his farm was in itself a healing, rewarding experience.

Solomon resumed teaching classes on a regular basis; some with Bob Black, others alone. Standing in front of English folks to teach a class didn't seem to violate Amish law, or the Bible, in this church district. Students paid a small registration fee to cover paperwork for each class held in his herb shop, which would easily accommodate seventy to eighty people.

The New Preacher did not interfere, nor did he voice an objection to the registration fee, or the classes Solomon and Bob Black taught in Ohio and Missouri, or anyplace else for that matter. Solomon even took a few promising students…those who insisted on learning more…under his wing by allowing them to study with him in the shop on a weekly basis.

All in all, things seemed to be going well for Solomon in his new location, until the New Preacher discovered he had paid cash for the 120 acres, that is. In addition to that disheartening discovery,

View of the homestead
Herb shop and office in foreground

The barn on the 120 acres

Solomon's Herb Shop & Office on the 120 acres

the Old Preacher convinced him that, because of Solomon's beliefs and strict morals, the man could be a threat to both his, and the New Preacher's authority, and to their way of life.

Suddenly, where Solomon was concerned, everything changed. The New Preacher seemed determined to prove to the Old Preacher that he could, and absolutely would, control Solomon Wickey by threat, or intimidation, or whatever means necessary to get the man under his pious thumb and keep him there.

The New Preacher recruited a few local Amish Comrades to act as vigilantes on the job twenty-four hours a day observing and reporting Solomon's every move. Yes, indeed, a man with a large family who could pay cash for 120 acres of good Adams County farmland would bear watching.

The New Preacher lived on a farm located on county road 100E, approximately one-half mile due west of Solomon. Their two farms were separated by a neighbor's eighty acres. Even with near perfect eyesight, Solomon couldn't see the New Preacher's house or barn at that distance through a stand of trees and thick underbrush dense enough to challenge the nimbleness of Br'er Rabbit, but the New Preacher seemed to have a clear, unobstructed view of everything going on at the Wickey place.

With the help of the Comrades he could, on any given day, recite the exact number of cars that came and went in Solomon's driveway, the number of packages the United Parcel driver dropped off and picked up, and how many cows the Wickey boys milked, how many cans of milk they sold every week, or the exact number of loads of loose hay Solomon and his sons hoisted into their haymow. The man was obsessed. He hardly had time to tend to the rest of his Amish flock, or provide adequate Biblical sustenance on Sundays.

186

The New Preacher's feisty little antics did not intimidate Solomon one iota. Even though he knew he was being watched Solomon made no changes in his own, or his sons', work or daily routine. Why should he? He wasn't doing anything wrong. Besides, he had made it perfectly clear to the preachers in both the old and new church districts that he refused to live under the rule, or control, of man. He lived under God's rules, he said, and had no intention of trying to please man over God.

While the New Preacher wasted energy trying to figure out how he could control Solomon, hundreds of people continued to spread stories through word of mouth about the miraculous work Solomon was doing, about how the lives of many whom medical doctors had assigned to death were being saved. Bobby G. was an example.

Bobby had open-heart surgery in 1989. The diagnosis: an atrial defect the size of a quarter between the left and right atrium of the heart.

The doctors very confidently told Bobby and his wife, Pat, that the surgery had been a complete success, and a speedy, full recovery was expected. It didn't happen. Instead, both Bobby's physical and emotional health deteriorated rapidly.

Pat's brother insisted that Bobby go see Solomon Wickey. He told Bobby that several people he worked with…people he and Pat had known since childhood…swore by Solomon, and went to see him regularly. He buttressed his argument by emphasizing the fact that each of them had a personal success story to tell.

Finally, after talking it over with Pat, Bobby decided to give Solomon a try. His situation was becoming more critical by the hour. He didn't have anything to lose.

Bobby sat down in front of Solomon with the attitude that, I'm nothing. There's nothing left in me. And, furthermore, I really don't believe you can help me.

As soon as Solomon looked into Bobby's eyes through an iridology glass he leaned back in his chair and said, "Your left eye tells me you have a hole in your heart."

"Had a hole in my heart," Bobby corrected. "HAD a hole! I'm recovering from surgery that repaired it."

"No, you DO have a hole in your heart. Now! Today!"

Bobby was stunned; shocked.

Perhaps it was the tone of Solomon's voice, or the confidence with which he spoke, or possibly deep down Bobby knew he spoke the truth. Whatever the reason, pent-up emotion erupted into a flood of tears streaming down his face as he looked at Pat and sobbed, "I'm gonna die. Pat, I'm gonna die! (More than twelve years later, emotion still filled Pat's eyes with tears every time she thought about the utter desperation they both felt at that moment).

To calm Bobby, Solomon asked in his usual quiet, soothing tone, "How long do you want to live?"

"Well, as long as I can," Bobby gasped between sobs.

"Do you want to live 'til you're sixty?"

"Well, yeah, I'd take that."

"How about seventy?"

"Yeah! Seventy would be good!"

Bobby wiped his eyes and blew his nose. Maybe he was actually going to walk out of there, because Solomon had just said he might live until he was seventy. Seventy! His seventieth birthday was still several years distant.

Pat asked Solomon what they needed to do to restore Bobby's health, and Bobby eagerly agreed to do everything Solomon suggested, including a strict diet and herb regimen. Solomon said it was a process. First, he explained, the herbs would line up the spine, and once that was done, would help the body to heal from the top down without side effects.

Pat pressed Solomon for a time. How long would all of that take, she asked? Days? Months? Longer? He remained silent, not wanting to answer, but finally after she kept insisting he ventured, "Well, maybe a year."

To satisfy her curiosity Solomon handed Pat an iridology glass and told her to find the dark spot at about three o'clock in Bobby's left eye. It looked like the head of a big straight pin, he told her.

Yeah! There it is!" she squealed when she found it.

Solomon explained to her that as the heart began to heal the spot would become smaller and smaller until it reached the size of a tiny pinpoint. At that time the hole would begin to weave. When the weaving process was complete, the hole would be fully closed. (That happened one year and two months later).

Pat bought an iridology glass that day to keep track of the weaving process, which began about Thanksgiving. By mid-February, 1990, Bobby felt wonderful. He went back to work. He dusted off his bass fiddle and rejoined the band he'd played with for thirty years. Life was good!

This, their first experience with Solomon, and with herbs, made believers of both Bobby and Pat. In their exuberance, they told everyone about the experience. Bobby insisted on seeing Solomon once a month for his own peace of mind, and since he was going anyway, taking another sick person, or two, along seemed like a good idea. Their new van filled quickly with people eager to make the trip.

Bobby was always behind the wheel. He loved to drive. They arrived at Solomon's office at eight o'clock for the first appointment of the day, and got back home in time for Bobby to clock-in on the second shift at the manufacturing plant where he had worked most of his life.

Word spread quickly as lives changed, and Pat and Bobby's phone began to ring. As a result, they were forced to block out an entire morning on Solomon's appointment book one day each month and take two vans in order to accommodate everyone who wanted to go along.

Over the years a strong bond of friendship was established between Bobby and Pat, and Solomon and his family. After thirty-eight years on the job, Bobby retired in good health. As one might expect, he had a few other health challenges along the way, but he trusted Solomon to deal with them...or occasionally one of his students, including Pat, who began studying with Solomon soon after Bobby retired.

Bobby G. came to love Solomon like a brother, and will as long as he lives. With Solomon perched in the front navigator's seat, Bobby and Pat enjoyed driving him and Anna Mae on numerous vacation trips, to meetings, to visit family and friends near and far, to go shopping, or just to go out to eat after a long day in the office. They became friends who simply enjoyed being together.

*****

To sustain their own loftiness and to influence the brethren against him, the New Preacher and his Comrades openly accused Solomon of practicing **witchcraft,** an unforgivable evil worthy of shunning. Shunning was one of the most dreaded punishments ever devised to keep errant Amish in line.

Some of the brethren bought into the accusation, but apparently they failed to convince God, because He continued to generously reward Solomon with a steady flow of revolutionary new information about how to eliminate all manner of illness that he continued to store in the private recesses of his mind, not a word of which was shared with anyone.

What was the purpose of this strange information being revealed to him when the need arose? What was he supposed to do with it? Solomon pondered the situation from every possible angle. He agonized over the rabid thoughts of those who construed his work as having anything to do with witchcraft. It was preposterous, as well as hurtful, for anyone to think he could be aligned with the Devil. The information he received came from God, of that he was certain.

Solomon constantly searched the Scriptures for answers and guidance. He lived by the conviction that he was only an instrument through which God worked to help suffering people. Everybody, even the most learned Christians, takes it for granted that the Bible's account of miracles Jesus performed could never happen today. But when the releases were followed exactly as given, the results begged no other Biblical comparison. The very thought that a force beyond the knowledge of man could be coursing through him was somewhat unsettling.

Solomon continued to use iridology and herbs, along with muscle testing, although he did not hesitate to use a release, if one came, to eliminate the originating cause of a serious problem. Even though the releases proved to be fast, as well as completely accurate, Solomon used them only when he was directed to do so. He doubted that most people were actually ready to accept the concept of an instant panacea, even though they might say otherwise.

Hard losers were still sending spies to look for even a tiny thread of evidence that Solomon was diagnosing, prescribing, or doing anything else that could be construed to be against the law. On one occasion they went so far as to send a man to beg for help, because, he said, he had an advanced form of AIDS. After testing him, Solomon told the imposter to go home, because he didn't have AIDS or anything else wrong with him.

As a result of such annoyances, Solomon worked with even greater caution than usual. Then, too, he didn't always know when the New Preacher or the Comrades were window peeping. They clearly didn't understand his method of testing, or the benefits of iridology and herbs. How could he expect them to understand the miracle of an instant remedy, when, at the time, he didn't fully understand it himself.

With the revelation of each new release, which came sporadically over a period of several years, Solomon prayed, and laboriously searched his soul to be sure God was its source. The response was always the same: **the human body was created to heal itself.** However, sometimes it needs an instruction, or command, in order to do so. When the release instruction is silently sent to the brain, it is then transmitted to the malfunctioning area in the body and carried out instantly; rather like the response when giving instructions to a computer with the click of a mouse, and hitting the delete button.

When God created the human body He gave it an inarguable intelligence far superior to that of any computer man will ever devise. Perhaps God was simply showing Solomon how to connect with that intelligence through the use of a release. Evidently He was trying to introduce a revolutionary new method of health care; something people would eventually be able to do for themselves. Solomon just didn't know that yet.

Without the faintest hint of malice, Solomon enjoyed life in spite of those few in his church district whose attitude toward him was filled with the stench of spite and hate. He laughed, yodeled, sang, played the harmonica and spoons, bred and sold registered Standardbred horses, attended equine sales around the Midwest, talked to lots of people, thoroughly enjoyed traveling, lengthy vacations, and the companionship of his growing family. By that time, five of his children had married, and precious grandchildren were beginning to arrive to bless and entertain him and Anna Mae.

One of Solomon's greatest pleasures was derived from watching a muscular, matched team of draft horses pulling a big hay wagon headed for the barn, piled high with fresh, air-dried alfalfa stuffed between the hayracks. He and his sons stored between seventy and eighty loads of loose hay in their barn every summer.

At the barn a giant hayfork dangling from stout, thick ropes looped through large wood pulleys, spread wide its cavernous jaws to grab great gobs of hay from the wagon. The hayfork was then hoisted to the second floor by horsepower, swung through a large door along a track in the barn's haymow, and guided to a place where it was tripped, letting the hay fall into a pile alongside the last load and spread out by men wielding pitchforks. It was a hot, scratchy job, but they hardly noticed, because to a farmer there is nothing quite as intoxicating as the smell of loose, new-mown hay. Solomon loved working in the haymow.

Anna Mae always brought mugs of hot tea to cool them off. Nothing cools one like a hot drink, and nothing ever tasted quite as good as her tea when they were hot and sweaty. Sometimes Solomon would take a harmonica out of his pocket to play while the boys laughed and teased each other, or threw their straw hats on the empty wagon and sprawled in the grass to rest before heading back to the hayfield for another load. Theirs was a wonderful, happy way of life that today remains only a memory to many.

As a way of saying thank you for saving the life of a loved one, a grateful gentleman who often came to the herb shop gave Solomon an unusual, intricately carved hardwood walking cane as a gift. Solomon proudly stood it in a corner of his office room to be admired and enjoyed by everyone. Soon other folks brought unusual canes to display, too. That was the beginning of his collection of rare and unusual walking canes, which, to date, number more than two-hundred, with only two duplicates. Solomon bought one himself, which he found at a flea market. It was ornately hand carved in Africa from a native wood. Very different! The others have been gifts from grateful people all over the world.

Speaking of people coming from all over the world...........

One warm sunny morning Solomon was startled to see a tall, dark skinned man shuffling barefoot across the gravel driveway toward the herb shop on wobbly legs, his body bent forward some forty-five degrees, precariously clinging to two stout caucasian gentlemen, one supporting him on either side. He was dressed in flowing pants topped by a rather long, short sleeved tunic fashioned of a fine, expensive grade of white linen rarely seen in the United States. He carried a pair of leather sandals, which later he admitted to wearing only when absolutely necessary.

Considering his unusually long legs, his helpers settled him into the chair in front of Solomon as best they could. In the most perfect, precise English he explained that he was a king from Africa. He said that as king he ruled as chief over five geographically separated tribes, with a wife, many children, and hundreds of warriors in each tribe.

He told Solomon that in an evil scheme to kill him his enemies had placed lethal poison on a running path they knew he would be traveling barefoot. Instead of killing him instantly by entering his body through the bottoms of his feet and moving up his spine on its way to his brain, the poison somehow became firmly lodged in his lumbar spine. Medicine men in Africa identified the problem, but considering the type of poison used, they didn't know how to remove it from his body. Granted, his life had been spared, at least temporarily, he said, but unless Solomon could help, he would surely be forced to spend the rest of his life dragging along on wobbly legs looking at the ground.

Solomon picked up an iridology glass and went to work. He found the poison lodged in the lumbar spine just as the medicine men said. Solomon very carefully tested, and re-tested, a variety of herbs before he was satisfied with the perfect combination that would clear the poison out of the king's body. Unexpectedly, though, while he was testing the herbs a release to remove the troublesome poison presented itself.

The king was overjoyed. For the first time in many months he could stand erect to his full height of eight feet. Solomon jokingly told him he'd never seen anyone whose feet were on the floor while at the same time his head touched the ceiling. The king said if Solomon thought he was tall he should've seen his father, who, at nine feet, was considered rather short in their village.

It was not everyday Solomon met a king; from Africa, or anyplace else for that matter. His visit was definitely a most enjoyable, entertaining occasion. Solomon leaned back in his chair and asked the king what brought him to the United States? To Adams County?

The king explained that the men with him were missionaries from Michigan assigned to work in one of the villages under his rule. Once they became aware of his predicament, they were thoroughly convinced that Solomon could help him, and agreed to bring him to the United States if he wanted to find out for himself. The three of them were on a plane as soon as travel arrangements could be made.

Solomon and the king continued their conversation as they walked outside together for a better look at the huge barn, whirling windmills quietly pumping water, Amish buggies, and twenty or twenty-five Standardbreds grazing in the pasture, all of which fascinated the king. The king was every bit as curious about Solomon's way of life as Solomon was about his.

He said that even though he was a king, he was not rich. The tribal kings in Africa are not rich, nor do they sit on a throne. Instead, they lead, protect and provide for their people, render judgment when disagreements arise, and always lead their warriors into battle if they have to go to war.

Before the king said goodbye, he gave Solomon a picture to remember him by. Dressed in official regalia, he was sitting in a palanquin, an ornate covered litter on poles being carried on the shoulders of four strong native bearers.

The king's visit was one of Solomon's all time most unforgettable. Later, in telling a friend about it, he laughingly said the king was so tall that when he walked through an ordinary door it looked like he passed through the eye of a needle.

*****

1987 was a year of significant change on all fronts throughout the world, particularly where individual health was concerned. The medical profession in the United States had long been at odds with chiropractors. In 1987 the chiropractic profession won a hard fought landmark case against the American Medical Association (AMA) for conspiracy to break the United States antitrust laws. This legal ruling successfully blocked the AMA from ever again trying to destroy chiropractors, or the chiropractic profession.

Solomon Wickey's vindication in the Adams County Circuit Court in 1983, served as a precursor to the antitrust ruling to protect a host of other healing arts and natural therapies from attack by the monopolistic AMA, thereby legitimizing them to step forward, to thrive and flourish.

In that same year, August, 1987, to be exact, mankind experienced the harmonic convergence, an undeniable force that propelled the earth and her inhabitants into a new era; an era devoid of mediocrity. In that tiny nanosecond when the planet stopped, and began anew, everything changed. Everything! Planet Earth had entered its transition into a new dimension; a new measurement of time. The incredible rush toward the new millennium had begun whether people were immediately aware of it or not.

By 1990, the new incredibly faster pace filled with unprecedented stress associated with a more competitive society zealously attached to such things as computers, cell phones, and multi-tasking, a generational label assigned to doing several things at the same time, had driven some people to near exhaustion. Among other things, they habitually took excessive amounts of medication, ignored their body's need for sleep, rushed through checkout lanes, and bought everything possible at drive-up windows, including food and drink, which, more often than not, they hurriedly consumed behind a wheel.

Home cooked meals lovingly served to families gathered around kitchen or dining room tables on a daily basis ceased to exist in many households. Few had time for such luxury, they said. Their criterion for food: it had to be fast, instant or frozen, and above all, microwaveable. After all, it was the 90s! Sadly, in a growing number of families, the occasional meals they ate together were at holiday feasts.

Manufacturers spent millions of dollars annually to advertise food and drink filled with man-made substitutes, synthetics, fat, sugar, aspartame, preservatives, empty calories, and more. Among some ideologies, people were becoming more concerned about protecting wetlands and endangered species than about taking care of their own bodies. Thousands reacted to the stress, neglect and poor diet by becoming ill.

Some people, particularly the younger generation, developed an affinity for living life at breakneck speed, whatever the cost. However, those with another persuasion preferred to live their lives quietly, more in harmony with the mysteries of nature, and through the art of gardening teach their children the benefits of all the plants nature so generously gave to mankind.

Perhaps the harmonic convergence was responsible, at least in part, perhaps not. But for those who were more intuitively and spiritually enlightened, the harmonic convergence brought a new awareness. They quickly lost patience with orthodox medicine's compulsive use of drugs to treat symptoms, but never looking for, or treating, the cause of a debilitating condition. Many were angry when, due to the abuse of prescription drugs, they had been left

198

to mourn celebrity idols such as Judy Garland, John Belushi, Elvis Presley, Marilyn Monroe, Dorothy Kilgallen, and many others.

Instead of risking the same fate, the more self-confident chose to circumvent traditional medicine and the dictates of health insurance companies, by taking control of their own health through holistic methods using herbs and nutrition. It was never their intention to wholly boycott the medical profession, but rather, to incorporate natural, less intrusive holistic methods into their health care regime. You can't depend on orthodox medicine if you want to live a long and healthy life, they said. You must take matters into your own hands by doing your homework and making your own decisions. It is your sovereign birthright.

The popularity of backyard gardens, farm markets and health food stores soared to new heights, while television screens were filled with antiseptic clad chefs touting the benefits of home cooking. Solomon's herb shop was busier than ever. He was forced to add new chairs in the waiting room to accommodate not only the English folks, but his Amish neighbors, as well.

Not everyone hated Solomon, or disagreed with his opinions. Those Amish people in his church district who loved, trusted, and admired him, routinely came to the herb shop to confer with him about their health problems, family problems, emotional problems, financial problems, or sometimes just to visit and share their joys, or a new joke.

The New Preacher did not have the willingness, or the ability, or the savvy, to understand Solomon, or the fact that he was one of the best known, most highly respected herbalists in the United States, or the importance of his work, or his acquiescence to the will of God by using, and growing, the talents he had so generously been given.

At every opportunity the New Preacher loudly proclaimed that Solomon Wickey had become much too worldly. Actually, the man was frightened of Solomon; frightened of his highly advanced spiritual perception, his quick mind; frightened of the power and influence he seemingly had, especially among his Amish neighbors.

The New Preacher thought people in his church district should bring their problems to him, not to Solomon, and he didn't hesitate for a moment to say so.

In the fall of 1992, the New Preacher paid an official visit to Solomon with orders to bolt the herb shop door, because, he shouted, the business was CLOSED!

But who can stand before jealousy?
Anger is cruel and fury overwhelming,

Proverbs 27:4

FOURTEEN

And God said Go.

Who? Me?

Yes, you.

But, God, I can't go.

I have people to see, things to do, places to be.

Do you love Me?

Yes!

Then go.

I went.

Author Unknown

Indeed, the casual observer might've thought Solomon only imagined the bird's song was sweeter, the frog's croak louder, the crisp, clean air easier to breathe, the sky a brighter shade of blue above thousands of huge, stately trees on that high ridge northeast of Madison in Jefferson County, Indiana, but to Solomon, who had nurtured a life-long dream of living among the trees in hill country, nothing could've been more real.

Even though it took great courage to leave the place of his birth and childhood memories, Solomon bought two-hundred-fifty acres of rolling, wooded land south of State Road 250 along narrow, twisting, hilly, graveled Scotts Ridge Road in the far northeast corner of Jefferson County about as far from the insults of Adams County as living in the great state of Indiana would permit.

His sons and sons-in-law quickly set about helping him build a large two story house on an idyllic knoll several hundred yards from a rather precipitous ravine eroded over time by rain water rushing to merge far below with the cool, clear, spring-fed water in Brushy Creek, one of the most remote, picturesque streams in Indiana.

They repaired and enlarged existing barns on the property to accommodate the livestock, the Standardbreds, and the draft horses. They also built several hundred rods of new fence, a spacious buggy shed, a new barn, and a woodworking shop to house Solomon's tools.

The new house and barns shared a gravel driveway with an existing smaller two story house out front. Standing only a few yards from Scotts Ridge Road, it served as Solomon's herb shop and office. The herb shop opened for business in March, 1993, a couple of days after he and his family moved into their new home.

For the first time since Frank Miesse introduced him to herbs and iridology, Solomon tackled the widely diverse physical conditions that walked through his door with an extraordinary new sense of freedom; freedom from the false accusations of the Wells County Health Department, the Indiana Attorney General's office, the Old Preacher, the New Preacher, the Troublemakers, the Comrades, and an Amish bishop from Ohio who, without Biblical justification, bought into their finger pointing and unsubstantiated accusations. Solomon left massive, deep, raw memories in Adams County where they belonged.

Solomon was a new man. He felt hundreds of pounds lighter. He laughed. He sang. He enjoyed the echo of his yodel bouncing from one hilltop to the next. His eyes sparkled. His step quickened. Happiness radiated from his soul. For the first time in his life he felt at home.

In his heart Solomon knew that God had led him away from his persecutors into this gloriously peaceful place. "If God wants you to do something," he said, "He'll make a way for it to happen."

In this case, God had some help. About two years earlier, three of Solomon's married children decided they'd had enough of the goings on in Adams County. Together with spouses and children, they found a more friendly Amish settlement in the vicinity of Pleasant, a tiny dot on the map near the Jefferson/Switzerland County line, where they established homes and made new friends. Thus, that same neighborhood was a logical destination for Solomon and Anna Mae.

Solomon and Anna Mae were thrilled to have several grandchildren living nearby, with new babies arriving every year. Because the nearest Amish community school was more than five miles away, and because educating their youngest sons and school age grandchildren was of such great importance to Solomon, he bought a parcel of land two miles, or so, north of his new place where the Wickey men erected a plain, no frills schoolhouse with a scenic three-mile view, separate outhouses, and a small, lumpy playground presided over by Amish teachers.

Once Solomon and his family moved out of Adams County his various persecutors directed their pent-up hostility toward Amish families who had supported him during his trial, and afterward. As punishment, each of those families suffered the stigma, the shame, of being shunned by friends and relatives, along with the ridicule and disgrace of being asked to leave the church district.

They scattered, settling into happier, more agreeable Old Order Amish church districts in Indiana, and elsewhere. Some of them bought and moved to farms a few miles from Solomon in the Jefferson/Switzerland County Amish settlement, and, like Solomon and his family, found peacefulness there.

Although to this day a handful of judgmental Amish brethren in Adams County have never been able to explain what Solomon and his supporters did to deserve such treatment, they have nonetheless solemnly vowed that their hearts will never again be open to them. Nodding in agreement, the New Preacher emphatically declared, "That door is closed, and it will stay closed!"

They refused to pay attention;
stubbornly they turned their backs and stopped up their ears.
They made their hearts as hard as flint and would not listen.
(Zechariah 7:11-12)

*****

Jefferson County's hilly terrain provided many happy new adventures and opportunities for the Wickey family. Solomon hired a contractor to build a lake along a secluded spot a fair distance behind the new house for the purpose of irrigation, he said, but smiled whimsically when he admitted it was well-stocked with fish even before it was fully filled.

He also built a large pond concealed from public view between the house and the lake, affectionately referred to by his grandchildren as the "swimming pond." A two-tier wood diving platform stood near the deeper water in the center of the swimming pond for the adults and older children, along with a long fiberglass slide that ended in shallow water close to the bank for the younger set.

The Wickey men built a shelter house along one grassy bank which they furnished with long picnic tables, lawn chairs, and oversized charcoal grills for spontaneous family gatherings. Solomon particularly enjoyed resting in a lawn chair in the open shelter house while being entertained by his younger grandchildren flailing their arms in the air above their heads as they flew down the long slide squealing and laughing, or playfully splashing in the water with their cousins and siblings.

The hills in southern Indiana also provided abundant new wintertime fun and adventure for a family accustomed to the flat land in northern Indiana, especially for the younger children who experienced the thrill of sledding down gentle knolls, or steep hills in the cleared pastures.

Without leaving their own land during the winter hunting season, the Wickey men and older boys...all expert marksmen... routinely provided a supply of fresh meat for the entire family by hunting quail, deer, rabbit, squirrel, and other wild game.

Yes, life in Jefferson County was good. Very good!

Solomon's mind was wide open to receive every good thing God sent his way. It should be no surprise, then, that the next ten years would prove to be the most productive, the most gratifying, of his career.

Solomon maintained the same work schedule in his new office: Monday, walk-in, Tuesday and Wednesday, by appointment. Before summer, people from all over the country had found their way to his new herb shop. Campers, large motor homes, and other vehicles filled with people eager to be among the first to see him Monday morning, began pulling into his driveway late on Sunday afternoons. Sometimes, especially on hot summer nights, the yard along Scotts Ridge Road in front of the herb shop resembled a campground when blankets and sleeping bags were unrolled on the grass next to coolers and baskets of food.

In the mists of pre-dawn people nervously congregated on the gravel driveway taking comfort in the camaraderie of others gathered there. While they waited for the herb shop to open, they shared scary medical diagnoses, anxieties, details of how they learned about Solomon, the distance they had traveled to see him, and endless stories about how previous visits had improved their own health, the health of family and friends, or, in numerous cases, saved their lives. The stories were the same every week, year in, year out. Only the storytellers changed.

Solomon's workload significantly increased as word of his new location spread throughout southern Indiana, southern Ohio, Kentucky, Tennessee, and beyond. Friends and relatives called loved ones in distant states with the news. They came.

Planes landing in Louisville and Cincinnati brought desperate people from afar, many of whom, according to medical diagnosis, should already be dead. Along with some pilots from Texas, others from Louisiana, Florida, California and Virginia flew, rented a car, and saw Solomon on a regular monthly, or bi-monthly, basis.

In the past, Anna Mae and the children living at home took turns working behind the counter in the herb shop, but as the children went to work or got married and moved away, more of the chore fell to her. Their two youngest sons, Joe and Ervin, shouldered much of the responsibility during the summer months, but when school started Anna Mae needed help. In September, 1994, she hired Delane, a woman who had been studying with Solomon, to work in the herb shop three days every week.

*****

Anthony and Joe were good friends. Even though they lived in the metropolitan area around New York City, they studied under Wendell Whitman, N.D. in Warsaw, Indiana, where each received his Doctor of Naturopathy (N.D.) degree.

In August, 1997, Dr. Whitman conducted a two-day week-end seminar in Warsaw, which Anthony and Joe, along with Anthony's wife, and two friends, attended.

During their years of study under Dr. Whitman, Solomon Wickey was quite often referenced as being the foremost authority in the United States on this subject, or that subject. Most of those attending the seminar knew Solomon personally, and spoke extensively about him; his wisdom, his knowledge.

Joe and Anthony simply had to meet this man, Solomon, this highly acclaimed herbal guru. So, armed with a letter of introduction from Dr. Whitman, and explicit directions, including a hand drawn map, they left Warsaw at the conclusion of the seminar Sunday night headed for Jefferson County.

They arrived at Solomon's place about two o'clock Monday morning, parked out by the gate, and slept in the car until they were awakened by vehicles pulling into the driveway shortly before daylight.

As soon as the herb shop opened Anthony and Joe rushed in to meet Solomon. They also met Anna Mae, and Delane, who was behind the counter, as well as Faye, one of Solomon's students. When they presented their letter of introduction, Solomon warmly welcomed them to sit in and watch him work for a few hours before they started back to New York. Not only did he graciously answer their questions, he also volunteered a great deal of valuable information.

A few weeks later, in mid-September, Anthony and Joe, along with their wives, went to Hawaii to attend a Nature's Sunshine convention. They unexpectedly ran into Faye there, and naturally their conversation turned to Solomon. Even though he did not voice his opinion at the time, Anthony thought it was utterly ridiculous when Joe asked her if she thought it would be possible for the two of them to study with Solomon. It was a crazy idea. After all, he reasoned, New York is not just around the next bend in Scotts Ridge Road.

Faye explained that there was usually a waiting list, but she seemed rather optimistic about the possibility, and promised to inquire for them. A few days after returning home, she called with the news that Solomon said it would be OK for them to come.

As soon as they could make arrangements to be away from their own offices for a few days, Anthony and Joe headed back to Indiana, found lodging in Madison, and were there, waiting, when Solomon opened his shop on Monday morning. Their education had begun!

For the next three days they sat in a corner taking notes, quietly observing and absorbing everything. Back at the motel in

Madison their evenings were spent comparing notes, discussing Solomon's methods, how he tested, the results he obtained, his mind set, and every other minute detail either of them could recollect about how he did things.

Joe and Anthony drove to Indiana one week every month for more than a year to study with Solomon. In the years thereafter, they made their study trips every other month.

In their own offices they each emulated Solomon as closely as possible, not changing a thing. Those things that worked so well for Solomon; his methods, testing procedures, confidence, attitude, etc., worked equally as well for them. He made everything so simple, so easy.

Thanks to Solomon, adverse health conditions will never intimidate either of them. Not ever! They know all illness is caused by some kind of imbalance in the body. When somebody comes in, even with the worst possible case scenario, Anthony and Joe carefully listen to their complaints, test that person to find out exactly what is going on, and quickly correct the problem.

Anthony spoke not only for himself, but also for Joe, when he said, "Solomon is a great man. I just thank God for meeting Solomon, and for him sharing so much with us.

"We learned a lot during the time we spent studying for the N.D. program, but there are things we learned from him we will never see in a book. We've learned so much. Oh, so much!

"I would call Solomon a researcher. There is always something new. After going there for so many years, every time we go back it's always exciting to see what's new, what are his latest discoveries, the things he looks for, or the way he approaches the body, and the new, or different, techniques he uses with people.

Scotts Ridge Road
A Centers photograph

Brushy Creek
A Centers photograph

The Swimming Pond
A Hanson Photograph

The Shelterhouse
A Centers photograph

"Oh, how great it has been to study with him. We are so grateful!"

*****

Melanie was another one of Solomon's more dedicated students in the new location. Initially, at the urging of her parents, she went to see him about a physical problem. Like so many others, she was in awe of the man, and of his work. So much so, in fact, that she asked how she could go about studying with him. "Read," he told her. "Read everything you can get your hands on regarding the human body and how it works."

Solomon knew she was serious when, after reading "The Chemistry of Man," which he had suggested as a good place to start, she showed up in his office week after week with long lists of thought provoking questions. He liked this petite, affable young woman who was starting from scratch. She brought a happy, bubbly breath of fresh air to his shop.

She had always kept a few basic herbs around the house, she said, but knew little about the scope of their usefulness, and of course, knew nothing at all about iridology.

Wednesday through Sunday, Melanie worked in a factory in a city about one-hundred-thirty miles from his shop, but for more than two consecutive years she studied with Solomon every Monday and Tuesday, and kept a standing Monday night motel reservation in Madison. She was determined to succeed. Her sights were set on helping people through a business and herb shop of her own.

Learning iridology was easy for her, but she found what Solomon called "releasing" more difficult. In all of her reading material she'd never found even a remote reference to the term. To help her understand, he explained that in addition to iridology, he

214

had shortcuts to release, and remove, a few specific malfunctions, which up to that time he had not shared with anyone. She was wide-eyed with excitement when he shared that information with her. Oh, wow, it was absolutely awesome!

In keeping with the technology generation...her generation... filled with passwords and personal PIN numbers, Melanie quickly dubbed his shortcuts as "codes." Thus, the term "release codes" was born.

*****

It is not unusual for medical doctors, a growing number who acknowledge that Solomon's expertise and abilities far exceed modern medicine and technology, to refer their patients to him. It was just such a referral that brought Jacque, a delightful, enthusiastic young woman, and Solomon together.

At the time, Jacque was enrolled in the certified natural health practitioner's program offered by Dr. Wendell Whitman's Trinity College of Natural Health, in Warsaw, Indiana. At the lecture podium, Dr. Whitman often spoke about his own experiences during the years he studied with Solomon Wickey, the man whom he considered to be the foremost authority in the United States on a wide variety of subjects pertaining to individual health and well being.

Jacque was jubilant when a medical doctor referred her mother to Solomon and gave her his address, because even though Dr. Whitman had liberally showered Solomon with high praise and appreciation, he had not divulged his whereabouts. Naturally, being eager to meet Solomon Wickey, she volunteered to take her mother to his shop. In fact, every seat in her van was filled that day with friends suffering health challenges.

215

They didn't have an appointment, but went early on a Monday morning, signed in, and waited their turn as do most people with a critical need. When their turn came, Jacque observed every detail as she sat beside her mother watching Solomon work. She didn't know how to apply, but one thing was very clear; she had to study with this great man, so on a sudden impulse she looked him directly in the eye and blurted out, "May I study with you?"

Her straightforward enthusiasm pleased him immensely. He grinned broadly, nodded as he stroked his beard, and without hesitation, said, "Yes!"

That was December, 1998. Since then she has been at his elbow at least two days every month. Continuing education!

Unlike a traditional classroom with a teacher, textbooks, assignments, tests, and fees, studying with Solomon is more of an observation and learn-by-doing experience. There are no stereotypes. Each case is different. The information filling his student's notebooks is of their own choosing.

Under Solomon's tutelage Jacque's large notebooks quickly bulged with hastily scribbled notes, but among them she did not have the answer to one of her most gnawing questions. She intuitively knew that occasionally Solomon used something beyond the limits of herbs and iridology to help people, but what was it? What?

She asked a zillion questions in pursuit of the elusive answer. Finally, when he felt comfortable doing so, he shared the information about how he released an adverse condition with her. He patiently explained that by silent, inconspicuous testing, the body's intellect would instantly reveal the exact origin of its own malfunction, as well as how to eliminate that condition by using a release code, an herb, or sometimes both. A release code, he said, merely acts as a catalyst to activate the healing power of an invisible force.

She didn't find the concept to be foreign or controversial in the least. Actually, she understood, and believed, everything he told her, knowing without a doubt it was true because, ironically, she had just been reading about this kind of thing in the Old Testament. The very idea that something so simple, painless and non-invasive could be the modern day answer to achieving optimal health only served to open a floodgate of other more demanding questions. In the weeks and months ahead, she constantly challenged Solomon, always wanting to know more. He loved it!

Granted, when there was a need, a code to release the condition automatically came to Solomon. But, she wondered aloud, if she asked would a code also come to her to release the malfunctions of someone she worked with in her own shop? Yes, Solomon said, it was possible to develop a release code for a specific need, although he rarely had to do so. By that time he had eight or nine codes, all committed to memory.

The concept excited and intrigued Jacque. By experimenting, she and Solomon found codes developed by using the information supplied by testing a person, to be entirely accurate. Sometimes a code was given exclusively for that individual person, but more often than not, it would release the same problem for others as well.

Once the secret was out Solomon not only felt a compelling responsibility, but also a sacred obligation, to share information about the release codes, and the results of their experiments, with his most dedicated students. The Scriptures clearly stated that one's God-given talents must be made to grow.

The Lord gave us wild strawberries for free.
No hoeing, no watering, no fertilizing.
They are just there for the taking.

*****

217

About that time another young woman, Katharine, began studying with Solomon on a regular basis, as did Jim, a well established osteopathic physician.

From the moment they met, Solomon knew Katharine was special. The powerful discerning light shining through her eyes told him so.

When she complained about not feeling up to par, her in-laws took her to see him. Solomon could fix anything, her father-in-law argued to persuade her to make the long trip to Jefferson County. Besides, he said, he liked Solomon; he trusted him. Of course he did. He'd known Solomon his whole life. They grew up on family farms in the same neighborhood near Berne, and as children they played together and attended the same public school. Forever friends.

Katharine was still in college studying dietetics at the time of her first visit, but later, after she graduated, she once again found herself traveling down Scotts Ridge Road on a personal quest to learn every aspect of pure natural herbs and their nutritional benefit to the human body. She could find no finer teacher than Solomon Wickey, Master Herbalist.

One or two days every week for almost three years she quietly sat in Solomon's office observing, listening, learning a multitude of things far beyond the understanding of her college professors. Not only did Solomon share his vast knowledge of herbs, their properties and their uses, with her, he also taught her how to "talk" to the body through quick, simple testing to find out exactly which herb, or combination of herbs, the body needed to repair the cause of the problem. Testing in this way eliminates all of the guess work, he said. Once she mastered the testing technique, she was on her way.

It is true that a mind once stretched by a new idea never returns to its original dimension. It is also true that the fundamental principle for maintaining excellent health throughout life is proper nutrition and pure natural herbs. They work, are affordable, and leave no troublesome side effects.

As far as Katharine was concerned, simply being in the room with Solomon was an empowering experience. A devout student of the Bible since childhood, she had many times read the stories about healing. Surely those things were reserved for Jesus when he was alive, and for Paul when he was teaching, she thought, but now, as an adult, she was watching similar miracles unfold. Studying with Solomon, she said, and watching him work with every imaginable illness, transformed Paul's teaching into a new understanding of what Jesus meant when He said, "And these things I do ye shall do also, and even greater things." There are no limits to possibilities.

Each person who studies with Solomon has a personal goal. They bring with them widely diversified backgrounds, different talents and abilities, and each is engaged in different work with people who have different needs. Most of them, like Katharine, are great humanitarians, although few can match her gentle compassion.

Unlike other students, Katharine filled her notebooks with information pertinent to herbs and nutrition, but along the way, she also became quite adept at iridology and releasing adverse conditions revealed by the eyes. She learned about the release codes, of course, but did not let them interfere with her primary focus; herbs and nutrition. The release codes, she concluded, are not a replacement for herbs and nutrition, merely an addition to.

In his quiet, unpretentious way, Solomon instilled in her a strong, proficient confidence that encouraged her to quickly identify a deficiency or malfunction, address it without hesitation, and move on, knowing it had been corrected.

Katharine was one of Solomon's all-time brightest and quickest students.

*****

For several years, Dr. Jim heard great stories from his patients about this Amish man, Solomon Wickey, and how he could "fix" things medical doctors overlooked, or gave up on, and he also heard that it was almost impossible to get in to see him.

Dr. Jim, an excellent physician with a curious mind, was always eager to learn everything possible about the human body. One day one of his patients casually mentioned that he had an appointment to see Solomon Wickey the following week. Dr. Jim said, "Oh, really? Well, I'd like to go along if I could."

Solomon was delighted to meet this quiet, soft-spoken medical doctor, and wasted no time in letting him know he would be welcomed back anytime. Dr. Jim was somewhat spellbound by everything he witnessed in Solomon's office that day. He had never seen anything like it before and definitely wanted to go back, but due to prescheduled events, it was a month, or so, before he showed up at Solomon's place again, notebook in hand.

At first, Dr. Jim sat quietly in a corner with Katharine, observing. He was especially impressed by how quickly Solomon located the core cause of a person's illness, which usually disproved a previous medical diagnosis. One of the first things Solomon explained to him was the method he used for testing, which in itself seemed simple. However, it took about two weeks of practice before Dr. Jim fully trusted his own accuracy.

For the next eighteen months he worked with Solomon every Monday and Tuesday viewing pathology from a different perspective. The broad spectrum of human ills coming into Solomon's office every day, and how he dealt with them so quickly and efficiently without benefit of so-called modern technology, was a totally new, thought provoking experience.

Solomon was beginning to be more comfortable, more confident, talking about the handful of release codes he had. He told Dr. Jim about them, and when the occasions arose, demonstrated how they work. Dr. Jim repeatedly watched people walk into Solomon's office with a serious illness and leave without it. He immediately recognized the undeniable, overwhelming power in the release codes. As he became acquainted with them, learned how to develop them, he wondered if Solomon fully comprehended the all-encompassing power in these release codes. They are extremely powerful!

Had the release codes come through traditional medicine they would've been heralded by the print and broadcast media as a great new breakthrough. But then, by the time most of the new medical breakthroughs...such as DNA...are ballyhooed, Solomon has already been working with them for several years.

Dr. Jim caught on quickly. In short order he was a pro at testing and using release codes, along with developing new ones. The idea of silently sending a message to a person's brain via a code that would almost immediately release and remove any derangement of their physical, mental or emotional health, regardless of its duration, intrigued him.

With some practice he was able to identify those problems as fast as Solomon; sometimes faster. Both Solomon and Dr. Jim checked the validity of the medical diagnosis. If it was correct,

Solomon would lean back in his big chair and let Dr. Jim find the release code if they didn't already have it.

More often than not, though, the diagnosis was way off the chart in the wrong direction. In that case, Dr. Jim quickly found the core cause of the problem, and developed a release code to fix it. Dr. Jim became lightening fast, and extremely accurate. Ultimately, he was responsible for developing the majority of all the release codes on the list.

Solomon was absolutely overjoyed to have Dr. Jim there. The energy, the excitement, in his office was at an all-time high. The two men were very comfortable working together. They became good, solid friends as respect, trust, admiration, camaraderie, grew steadily between them.

"Solomon taught me things I won't realize for years to come," Dr. Jim said. "He is wonderful; so refreshing. He encourages everybody to try to learn to do what he's doing. He has gone through so many stages and phases in his work. That's what you have to do in your evolution."

Dr. Jim and Solomon shared knowledge and expertise freely, one with the other, as well as numerous jokes. Solomon tells funny, clean jokes all day long as if that's all he has to do. In addition to enjoying good jokes, they also serve a useful purpose. Laughter not only relaxes the person sitting in front of him, particularly those with debilitating diseases, it also breaks up his own stress in constantly dealing with those critical situations.

Dr. Jim joyfully shucked his studious, serious professional persona when he was with Solomon, revealing his own incomparable sense of humor. More often than not, Solomon and Anna Mae, along with the students who wanted to go, went to Solomon's favorite restaurant in Madison for a meal after the door closed behind the last customer every Monday. It was a relaxing evening of jokes, laughter, and fun for all. Dr. Jim, Bobby and Pat were regulars.

*****

Thanks to Dr. Jim, new release codes were coming so fast that it was hard for Solomon to keep up with them, so he simply jotted them down on scraps of paper, stuck them in a drawer until he needed them again, and went on to the next person coming through the door. But help was on the way. Enter Roger.

Roger's wife, Hazel, had an unusual eye condition that refused to respond to conventional treatment. A co-worker gave her detailed directions to Solomon's place and encouraged her to go see him. For one reason or another, Hazel never seemed to find a convenient time to make the trip from Ohio to Jefferson County.

Finally, as her eye condition worsened, Roger put Hazel, daughter, Bridgett, and his in-laws into the car and headed for Jefferson County. They took their chances by going early on Monday morning and waiting their turn. It was a rewarding trip for all concerned.

After observing the way Solomon worked, Bridgett was determined to study with him. However, at that time she was doing her college prerequisites for a physical therapy degree and couldn't sandwich trips to Jefferson County into her schedule. But, as daughters often do, she came up with a plan.

She reasoned that since her dad's work was fairly flexible, he should go in her stead. After listening to his daughter talk about it non-stop for the next two years, Roger finally agreed to sit in with Solomon and take notes for her.

He went as often as his own work schedule and vacation days allowed. Naturally he met all of the regulars, and other students as they came and went, learned about the release codes, and saw Solomon's hand scribbled list which, quite honestly, he found hard to decipher.

Solomon decided that Roger, being a happy, intelligent, accommodating chap, was just the person he'd been looking for to take charge of the code list and keep it up to date. Even though Roger rather reluctantly agreed in the beginning, he did an outstanding job with this difficult task He consistently up-dated the list twice a year, but added new release codes only after he and Solomon or Dr. Jim checked, and double checked, each of them for accuracy. Each release code on the list was developed for a specific person who came to Solomon, or to one of his students, bringing the diagnosis from his or her own medical physician.

His first printed list consisted of only four or five pages. Six-hundred-fifty-eight release codes, covering almost every human disorder one can think of, filled about twenty-five pages less than three years later.

Roger was an excellent steward of the work. He kept tight control by producing the exact number of copies of the code list that Solomon authorized, although an unauthorized person wouldn't know what it meant, or what to do with it, if he or she somehow fell heir to a copy. Those few who are privileged to have a copy, honor Solomon by keeping it confidential.

*****

Solomon watched the big motor home bearing a Tennessee license plate pull into his driveway. It was Sherman and Jan. For the past year, they came from the vicinity of Nashville, Tennessee every Sunday evening so Sherman could study with Solomon Monday through Wednesday.

Sherman was an interesting fellow; one Solomon always looked forward to seeing. He had great stories of a long military career to share; stories Solomon never grew tired of hearing. Solomon referred to him as "The Military Ambassador."

The ROTC program sent Sherman to the United States Air Force directly after he graduated from Purdue University with a degree in animal science. (He entered college as a pre-med student, later changed to animal science). He proudly served as captain in the Air Force, but after one particular four-year stint of active duty he felt a strong call to preach, and transferred to the Air Force Reserves so he could attend classes at the seminary. He got his masters degree in religion, then his Ph.D. in divinity. He pastored a church and was ordained, but a technicality prevented him from serving as a chaplain in the Air Force.

Sherman resigned his commission in the Air Force and enlisted in the United States Army as a chaplain with the rank of colonel. After he retired from the Army, he and Jan moved to Indianapolis to be near their son, and began their own evangelism ministry.

Bill, his son's father-in-law who also lived in Indianapolis, underwent every known medical treatment for cancer, and after an unsuccessful surgery, was told he had only a few months to live. When Bill decided to give alternative medicine a try, he invited Sherman to go with him to see Solomon Wickey. With Solomon's help Bill lived another four years. Before he died he told Sherman he felt certain that had he gone the holistic route in the beginning he would have lived to be a healthy old man.

Sherman was terribly impressed with Solomon, and with his approach to achieving optimal health. He wanted to find out more about this man and the work he was doing, so he made arrangements to study with him. Sherman didn't always sit quietly on the sidelines as did most other students. Instead, he many times bantered back and forth with Solomon, sharing knowledge, learning through questions and answers.

He and Solomon agreed that the body doesn't malfunction because of just one thing. Two, three, or more things connect before a malfunction occurs, and it is important to find out what all of those things are. Solomon often says, "The body heals like an onion peels…layer by layer."

It is a foregone conclusion that conventional medicine focuses on symptoms instead of prevention; on the effect, not on the cause. In his book, "The Pulse Test," Arthur Coca, M.D. said, "I am a realist. As long as the profit is in the treatment of symptoms rather than in the search for causes, that's where the medical profession will go for its harvest."

Solomon and Sherman engaged in long discussions about how finding the cause of an illness will lead to its prevention, and agreed that the body functions the way it does because it is a spiritual element. "Spiritual elements can never be proved scientifically," Sherman said.

Sherman gratefully embraced the blessing of the release codes, which he found to be Biblically sound, and he had great success in using them to help people.

Speaking of Solomon, Sherman said, "I like that man. I love his approach, and his spirit of humility is just fantastic. He's not a showman. He is strictly genuine and sincere, every bit a gentleman from sole to crown. He doesn't do anything for show.

I've seen him pray for people. I've seen him cry for them. He does not advertise. He says it works out better if you let people come to you. I use that same approach in my ministry."

Hundreds of people have studied with Solomon throughout the years; the truly dedicated for months and years on end; others, only a day now and then. But in this day of his highest achievement, Solomon literally burst with pride when fervent professionals like those mentioned here wholeheartedly sanctioned his work by playing a vital role in the birth and expansion of the release codes. Their diverse backgrounds lent a dimension of credibility to the endeavor that would have otherwise been impossible. He will forever be grateful.

**In the right formation, the lifting power of many wings
can achieve twice the distance of any bird flying alone.**

The political climate in the United States changed drastically during the 1990s, as did health care. The stock market remained bullish. People who wanted an opulent lifestyle spent lavishly for everything they wanted, or thought they wanted, including rich, fattening food. Dieting and fitness centers were very much in fashion.

Insurance companies raised health insurance premiums significantly, forcing many people into health maintenance organizations (HMOs), some of which went bankrupt, leaving thousands of policyholders without affordable health care insurance.

Pharmaceutical companies introduced an untold number of new prescription and non-prescription drugs, most of which became household words through television and print media promotional advertising. Huge new hospitals and medical facilities popped up faster than a politician's promises, while costly new medical technology dived into everything; laser surgery, joint replacements, organ transplants, artificial insemination, cloning, and ever so much more.

In spite of the huge amount of money being spent on diets, exercise equipment, new drugs, state-of-the-art facilities, technology, etc., not only were more people sick, they were sicker than ever before. More and more of them chose to bypass conventional medicine by taking charge of their own health through the use of herbs and alternative medicine. The 1990s will long be remembered as the decade for alternative medicine's rebirth in North America.

Alternatives were no longer considered to be out on the fringes, but became highly legitimate, financially significant elements of prudent health care. A growing number of Americans who were dissatisfied with the care they received from established medical sources sought treatment...without the knowledge of their physicians...from a wide range of alternative providers. This trend focused more attention on Solomon and the work he was doing.

Unbeknownst to Solomon, one woman, in her exuberance and gratitude for his help in restoring her health, intercepted people going into a medical facility in her city, put them in her van, and drove them to see him. They, in turn, sung his praises to everyone who would listen.

It was not unusual for people to go crowing to their medical doctors about how Solomon had fixed an on-going problem of long standing. Angry and dismayed when a new bevy of tests could not locate the previously diagnosed problem, the medical doctors sent scathing letters to Solomon demanding copies of both his laboratory test records and his prescribed treatment for "their mutual patients." Solomon did not respond.

Throughout the years hundreds of people have studied with Solomon, but the students who attended his classes or lectures on herbs and iridology in Adams County, or those who just sat in with him occasionally, were not necessarily privy to information about the powerful release codes.

One of those students opened her own herb shop in a small west central Indiana town. When Mrs. Occasional Student ran into a particularly stubborn case that refused to respond to the herbs she recommended, she sent the man to Solomon. Solomon quickly located the man's problem, and without comment or discussion, directed a release code to fix it. Once done, he asked, "Is there anything else?"

"No."

"That's it then," Solomon said as he leaned back in his big chair.

The man was furious. He couldn't get home fast enough to call Mrs. Occasional Student to complain, because, he said, he made the trip for nothing. Solomon only spent about five minutes with him, and didn't do anything for him. He didn't look in his eyes, or recommend a different herb. Nothing!

To soothe his ruffled feathers, Mrs. Occasional Student opened her herb shop after hours so he could get a couple of herbs she hadn't already tried. Miraculously, by the next day he was feeling much better, and lo and behold, there has never been a reoccurrence of the problem. It is gone. His medical doctor cannot find a trace of it. The man swears that the woman, not Solomon Wickey, is an absolute genius.

Mrs. Occasional Student now enjoys a self-proclaimed reputation of being ever so much better than Solomon Wickey. She doesn't study with him anymore. No need to.

Dedicated students who studied with Solomon for extended periods of time rarely have an opening in their appointment books. Some of those who only studied with him briefly, on the other hand, use Solomon's name to generate business without his consent or knowledge. Some of them take the liberty of placing large yard signs in front of their businesses, boldly emblazoned: **STUDIED WITH SOLOMON WICKEY.** Then there are those who print **Studied with Solomon Wickey** on their business cards, or in newsletters or flyers, and even a few who advertise their businesses on the Internet, claim to be a **Protégée of Solomon Wickey.** Caveat emptor!

*****

Solomon's personal life was happy, busy, and full of change. Silver began replacing the dark strands in his hair and beard. Eyeglasses became a necessity. He pridefully bragged of having nine beautiful new grandchildren born in a single month. He was fascinated by cell phones ringing in people's pockets or purses, and even more fascinated when a student put one to his ear.

As an Amish man, Solomon does not vote, nor does he participate in partisan politics, although sometimes he has a very strong personal opinion about political matters. Even so, in addition to people filling his waiting room seeking help for physical problems, investors, businessmen, and politicians of every persuasion, regardless of whether they sought a seat on the county council or in congress, came to his door one by one, seeking his advice, his endorsement, and/or money. Oh, if only walls could talk!

Solomon's faith is, indeed, extraordinary. On a warm, sunny day in late September, he looked out his office window just in time to see his intended Thanksgiving turkey heading down the driveway toward Scotts Ridge Road. He told Faye, who was sitting there taking notes, "Quick, go send that turkey back to the house. He's not fat enough to eat yet."

She jumped up, laid her pen and notebook on her chair and exclaimed, "Oh, what'll I do?"

"Just tell him I said to go back to the house," he replied matter-of-factly.

Out in the driveway Faye spoke to the turkey in her soft Kentucky drawl as she slowly waved her hands in the direction of the house. When she told the gobbler that Solomon said to go back to the house before it got killed on the road, he stopped, looked at her, turned around, fanned his tail feathers, and strutted back to the hen yard behind the house.

Another day, when someone yelled through an open office window to tell Solomon the horses were out, he ran outside, raised his hand, and told those huge draft horses with hooves pounding straight toward him, to go back through the gate they had somehow opened. They did. He slowly walked up there, closed and locked the gate, then went back to an office full of people just like it was an everyday occurrence.

Due to the hugely increased volume of motorized traffic on Scotts Ridge Road between State Road 250 and Solomon's place, the Jefferson County Highway Department blacktopped that portion of the road. Solomon had part of the driveway adjacent to his herb shop blacktopped as well, and laid down a concrete parking lot, complete with a basketball goal at one end next to the pasture where he kept Congou, his prized Standardbred stallion.

It was quite an honor to own this horse, son of Valley Victory, one of the most famous Standardbred stallions in the United States. Congou was sired and raised in Canada. Solomon bought the horse in Delaware, Ohio, after Leonard A. died, shortly before he moved to Jefferson County.

Solomon Wickey has always been a well-known, highly respected horseman. When word got around that he had a special gift for treating them, it was not unusual for large trailers bearing ailing horses…some from great distances...to pull into his driveway on Saturday mornings seeking his help. If a horse was not able to travel, he would oftentimes go to it.

For example, early one morning a stranger came looking for Solomon. The man said he had a sick horse which the veterinarian wanted to put down, and asked Solomon if he would take a look at it. Solomon agreed.

The man took Solomon to a big horse barn on his farm in the heart of The Bluegrass near Lexington, Kentucky, where he kept racing stock. Solomon quickly found the cause of the Thoroughbred's ailment and, using a code, released it immediately. Once the horse was back on its feet, the grateful man drove him back to Jefferson County. It was a beautiful day. Solomon enjoyed the trip.

For an Amish man without a motorized vehicle, Solomon was extremely well traveled. He loved vacations, and planned at least one every year. In addition, there were trips from both Nature's Sunshine and PURE HERBS LTD. given in appreciation of his outstanding annual sales.

Choosing an appropriate gift for Solomon demanded creative thinking on the part of both companies. One year the folks at Nature's Sunshine gave him a fine new family buggy in lieu of the shiny new Cadillac they had advertised as top prize. Another time they gave him a beautiful, solid oak grandfather clock to adorn his living room.

On another occasion, Nature's Sunshine's sales department arranged for Dr. Eugene Hughes and his wife, Kristine, to take Solomon, Anna Mae, and their sons who were living at home at the time, on a wonderfully relaxing riverboat trip down the Ohio River between Madison, Indiana, and Louisville, Kentucky.

As they floated down the river's deep center channel, Solomon played the harmonica while his sons played the spoons, and together, they harmonized in song, reminiscent of nineteenth century travelers making the same journey.

The excursion included passing through locks along the way, touring a baseball bat factory in Louisville, and an afternoon with the horses at Churchill Downs. It was a most memorable occasion for Eugene Hughes. Not only was he royally entertained by the Wickey family musicians, he also enjoyed visiting in Solomon's home, and riding in his buggy.

Dr. Eugene Watkins at PURE HERBS LTD. solved the reward problem by giving his top salesmen an all expense paid trip to the company's annual convention, which was held in a different location each year. Since the Amish don't fly, Bobby and Pat usually chauffeured Solomon and Anna Mae, and were graciously included in the convention festivities.

Gatlinburg, Tennessee, and San Antonio, Texas, were among Solomon's favorite PURE HERBS convention destinations. Gatlinburg, because of its beautiful mountain scenery, and because it was there that he saw his first live bear; a black bear. San Antonio, because of a comprehensive, graphic tour of the Alamo, and a spectacular moonlight dinner-cruise aboard a flat-bottomed barge poled by a single, brightly dressed oarsman as it snaked through the heart of the city along the famous San Antonio River Walk's

233

dramatically lighted business district. The food, as well as the scenery, was outstanding

As a side trip, Bobby and Pat took Solomon and Anna Mae to Corpus Christi so Solomon could see the Gulf of Mexico and play on Padre Island for a few days before heading up the gulf coast toward Houston and Baton Rouge, then northward to Indiana; another wonderful adventure to file away in his memory.

Horse and tractor pulls were becoming increasingly popular among farmers at regional and county fairs all across rural Indiana. In the spirit of competition, young Amish men, including Solomon's sons, enthusiastically joined in by organizing their own pulls to be held each Saturday afternoon at a different Amish farm. These young men pitted their biggest, strongest draft horses against each other, confident that his could pull the 8,000 pound sled the greatest distance in spite of its tremendous resistance.

It became great summertime entertainment for entire Amish families who went along to cheer, and, of course, wherever Amish folks gather, there, also, is abundant food. In this case, the pulling contests quickly became known as "the chicken pulls."

These occasions were great neighborhood fun, especially for the older Amish men like Solomon and his generation who knew good horse flesh when they saw it. They became every bit as competitive as their sons.

Solomon rearranged his work schedule so he and his sons could attend the big regional horse auction held in Columbus, Ohio every February. He bought the perfect horse, a huge, muscular Percheron; their new pulling champion!

Solomon's office became a virtual beehive of activity with new students from every walk of life coming from several surrounding states to study with him. Perhaps news of the release codes brought them, or perhaps it was simply their knowingness that the golden age of herbs and nutrition had begun and they wanted a seat on the bandwagon. Pat was different. She had become a perpetual student-helper of sorts, because through the years she and Bobby just loved being there. While she sat in with Solomon, Bobby busied himself by visiting with people, mowing Solomon's grass, gathering stones from Brushy Creek to border a flower bed in his yard at home, or driving Anna Mae and the boys here and there to do errands.

Occasionally, someone with a less than honorable motive was still being sent to spy on Solomon, and he consistently ignored their continued efforts to silence him. He instinctively recognized a spy the moment he, or she, walked into his office, and routinely verified his suspicion by simply asking their body, which never lies, and dealt with them accordingly. The spy organization still thought they could fool him. They were so far behind.

A particularly nasty, bitter spy came in one day loudly denying a belief in God, spewing vengeful, hateful drivel, accusing Solomon of witchcraft, and worse. His was definitely not the attitude of a happy, healthy person.

Solomon endured the nasty barrage for a few minutes before quietly telling the man he couldn't talk like that in his office. The man quite indignantly got up to leave, arms churning, brow furrowed over squinting eyes above taut, puckered lips that moved accusingly, but not a sound came out of his mouth. He railed at everyone as he stomped through the waiting room toward the door, mouth moving, lashing out, but not a sound did he make as he left the premises. It was one of the more entertaining moments for Solomon, his students, and those in the waiting room, as well. Perhaps it was his good friend, the Devil, who silenced him. Do you suppose?

By contrast, one Monday a middle-aged woman with a hugely extended abdomen was observed resting on a makeshift bed in the back of a van bearing an Illinois license plate. She lay there from early morning until late afternoon, patiently waiting to see Solomon, and when her turn came she was carried into his office on an improvised stretcher. About thirty minutes later, she slowly walked back to the van assisted by a male family member.

Even though Solomon rarely, if ever, tells anyone to come back, early the following Monday morning the same van pulled into his driveway, carrying the same woman. Improvement was obvious. Not only had her abdomen returned to its normal size, she also sat in a normal upright position in the car seat, and walked into Solomon's office unaided. She returned of her own volition just to thank him, and make sure all traces of the problem were gone.

A high percentage of those coming to Solomon for help were babies and young children with unusual or abnormal conditions, many of which were caused by the birthing process. Baby shots induce more distress for them than anything else, with the oft medically diagnosed attention deficit disorder with hyperactivity (ADHA), ranking as the number one perpetrator. When he tested them, one child's body after another told him the same story; syringe needles accidentally puncturing their tiny nerves, encapsulated drugs trapped there, unable to escape. Once Solomon released all foreign substances from the nervous system, those same little tyrants immediately turned into calm, peaceful, well behaved children as grateful parents watched in awe.

Solomon has been responsible for concocting more than a dozen herbal, and herbal combination, formulas. One, a formula he and his nephew developed for a child, is described by Dr. A. B.

Howard in his book, **Herbal Extracts: Build Better Health With Liquid Herbs**.

I.V.Y.-D: The combination of Iris, Violet, and Yarrow, (I.V.Y.) is the product of trust in the providential association of these three flowers as called attention to by a child named Danny, and confirmed by Solomon Wickey and Jake Schwartz, two great living Amish Herbalists. Use to reverse the modern scourge of AIDS, and many other contagious types of "dis-eases."

Dr. Howard describes another of Solomon's formulas in the same book:

CAN-SOL: Kills stubborn yeast infections. This unique combination was designed and formulated by the much loved and admired, living Amish Herbal Practitioner, Solomon Wickey, for severe cases of Candida and other persistent yeast infections.

One day, a terribly distraught man came to Solomon asking for help. He said his wife was going to leave him, and confessed that he was sure it was because he was no longer as sexually active as he'd once been. He was convinced that the only way to win her back was by increasing his sexual stamina, but instead of the expensive new widely advertised little blue pill for men, he said he wanted an herb; something safe and effective without adverse side effects.

Solomon did what he could for the man, and he left. Just as he walked out to his truck an herbal formula popped into Solomon's head, and he knew instantly it was the perfect answer to the man's problem. The man drove away in spite of several people trying to stop him, so he did not benefit from "his" formula, although hundreds of others have.

When Solomon painstakingly tested the new formula, he found that it would be just as effective for women as for men.

He immediately sent the formula to Dr. Watkins at PURE HERBS LTD. where, after thorough testing, it was named S.M.&W.-

237

S (Sex for men and women by Solomon) and added to the product line with the following description:

S.M.&W.-S. This herbal extract is more than just a hormone replacement. It balances the whole body, particularly the hormonal field. Once the body is rebalanced, it will act on its own to produce sufficient hormones.

As pure-quality herb companies continued to grow and prosper in the United States, threatening established drug monopolies, the pharmaceutical companies united in a strong push to take control of herbs, vitamins, minerals, and dietary supplements under the wing of the Food and Drug Administration by influencing Congress to pass new federal laws allowing the FDA to exercise unprecedented authority over these all-natural products, but they were not successful.

Mother Nature is wiser than all of the pharmaceutical companies put together. Medical doctors know little, if anything, about herbs. They don't know how to use them, and above all, they don't know the benefit of pure-quality herbal products versus synthetics found in most drug stores. The orthodox medical profession's version of preventative medicine is vaccination, so they're learning about the healing properties of natural solutions at a snail's pace, if at all.

Because Solomon was widely known as an expert master herbalist, he was invited to go to Washington, D.C. to speak to the United States Congress on behalf of the pure-quality herb companies, and also to lobby on behalf of American consumers' sovereign right to chose when it comes to their individual health and the health of their children. He declined the invitation, but looking back, wished he had gone.

Solomon found himself looking back at some other things, too. Important things!

He was so happy living in his beautiful hill country that he failed to notice that his passion was not shared by all. In a weak moment, Anna Mae confessed that she really wanted to go back home. It was not that she didn't like Jefferson County. She loved her house and having some of her children and grandchildren close by, but she missed living closer to her daughters, and sorely missed the companionship of her sisters and brothers as they grew older.

Solomon had some serious thinking to do. Anna Mae was a good wife. None could've been better. She gave birth to thirteen children, raised twelve. He'd often said she did the work of ten; never stopped. She cooked, cleaned, hung laundry outside to dry every day, planted flowers, and canned the bounty of a large garden to feed her family through the winter. She made clothes for the entire family, including her husband. She stood by him through the court trial, through all of the false accusations hurled at him by the Old Preacher, the New Preacher, the Troublemakers, the Comrades, and endured the shunning. She watched eleven of her children marry, and welcomed each new grandchild. She had always managed the herb shop, ordered product, paid the bills, packaged and sent out mail orders every day, did the banking, met with the tax accountant, and more things than he could count.

For the past ten years he had lived in his own utopia. Now, he decided, it was time to take Anna Mae back home. She deserved it.

Solomon immediately started the ball rolling. First, he and Anna Mae discussed the matter with all of the children. They made several trips to northern Indiana looking for available land in a suitable location. Amish customs and traditions are sacred to each

239

of them, so before they made an offer to purchase the parcel they preferred, they went to see the Amish bishop presiding over that church district.

In this bishop they found a man with the wisdom to appreciate Solomon's God-given talents, as well as why, and how, he used them to help people according to Divine direction.

Solomon was very frank and straightforward in telling the bishop about his problems in Adams County. After listening intently, asking and answering questions, the bishop graciously welcomed Solomon and Anna Mae and their family into his church district.

The property they chose was 160 acres of unimproved level production farm land running along a gravel road in DeKalb County north of the Allen County line, not far from her birthplace. To establish new homesteads for themselves and some of their sons who would also be moving, they would have to start from scratch, submit plans to the county plan commission for large houses, big barns, tool sheds, spacious buggy sheds, and a long building to accommodate the herb shop in one end, with a kitchen and space for family and church gatherings in the other end. They would have to comply with county zoning rules, get building permits. Everything!

Since a municipal water line ran along the road in front of their chosen home site, they could have running water, a standard bathroom in both the house and the herb shop, and solar power. Solomon Jr., upon whom they had always depended heavily, would be in charge of this huge undertaking.

Back in Jefferson County, the move was the main topic of conversation. In addition to keeping his regular schedule in the shop and making almost weekly trips to DeKalb County, Solomon posted a For Sale sign, and arranged for an auction sale.

Solomon's days were filled with both joy and sadness. He was genuinely touched by all of the students, and the crowds of people that loved and appreciated him who came from a distance to thank him for sharing his talents so freely, for saving their lives or the lives of loved ones, to shower him with mementos straight from their hearts, to wish him well in the new location, and, for some, to say goodbye. One couple, Ron and Mary Ann gave him an especially meaningful gift to cherish.

Mary Ann, who had studied with Solomon for some time and dearly loved him, along with her husband, Ron, a professional photographer, arrived at Solomon's place early one morning in late October armed with cameras and tripods. They spent the entire day roaming the property, taking pictures of everything Solomon held dear; his fishing lake, the swimming pond, waterfalls and ripples in Brushy Creek, trees dressed in fall colors, wild flowers, horses, barns, fences, the county road, the house, the herb shop. The portfolio containing an enlargement of each beautiful picture was the perfect nostalgic gift.

Solomon left his beloved home in the hills of Jefferson County on November 14, 2002, his sights set on grand new adventures, including his long-time aspiration to lecture extensively on herbs, and to raise quail. And then, too, there was another long-time dream of taking an extended trip to Alaska, but not on a tour bus. He wanted someone like Doug Clower to drive him so he could sit up front, play with binoculars, read comic books, tell jokes, fish, and take numerous side trips along the way.

Ah, the dreams of a modest man; one of God's most magnificent!

Success

He has achieved success who has lived well,
laughed often and loved much;
Who has enjoyed the trust of pure women,
the respect of intelligent men
and the love of little children;
Who has filled his niche and accomplished his task;
Who has left the world better than he found it,
whether by an improved poppy,
a perfect poem or a rescued soul.
Who has never lacked appreciation of
earth's beauty or failed to express it;
Who has always looked for the best in others
and given them the best he had;
Whose life was an inspiration;
Whose memory a benediction.

Written by
Bonnie Anderson Stanley
in 1904

The family home
A Hanson photograph

Solomon's herb shop / office
A Hanson photograph

Brushy creek
A Hanson photograph

Solomon's place
A Centers photograph

246

Down Sugum Hollow Road
A Centers photograph

Brushy creek
A Hanson photograph

EPILOGUE

Historically, when God decides to send the inhabitants of planet earth in a new direction, He sends a messenger, or sometimes an entire army of them, to lead the way. In this instance, messengers were sent to herald a natural approach to taking care of the human body.

Solomon J. Wickey is one of those carefully chosen messengers; not the only one, to be sure, just the most recent of those we will discuss here.

Although each messenger has delivered the same identical message, each has presented it in a different way, and since God won't be denied, we can expect legions of new messengers shouting with even stronger voices until mankind finally "gets it."

*****

Edgar Cayce, one of the great legends of our time, was among God's most notable messengers. Cayce was born on a Revolutionary War land-grant farm near Hopkinsville, Kentucky, March 18, 1877. Known as the "sleeping prophet," he encouraged people to open their minds to achieving optimal health through a variety of natural substances and modalities, all of which were alternatives to

249

conventionally accepted medical practices of that day. He taught that, ultimately, healing is self-generated.

According to his father, Leslie Cayce, known around town as "the Squire," Edgar was a dull student; a dreamer, slow to learn. One night when the Squire was helping his twelve-year old son with spelling homework he became terribly discouraged when the lad couldn't spell a single word on the list. Edgar insisted it was because he was too sleepy, and convinced his dad that if he could just sleep for a few minutes he knew he could do better.

After sleeping with his head on the spelling book for not more than five minutes, Edgar, wide awake and full of excitement, could spell every word on that week's list, as well as the words on every other spelling list in the book, too. After that night he slept on all of his lessons, knew all of them perfectly, and for as long as he lived, he not only remembered, but could recite verbatim everything he learned while he was asleep.

Edgar began having severe headaches shortly after he took a job as a traveling salesman in February, 1900. To alleviate a particularly violent headache, a small town physician on his route gave him a measure of white powder, with orders to take it with a glass of water.

That evening one of the Squire's friends who had been visiting in that same small town found Edgar wandering around in a foggy daze, and took him home where he was ordered to bed by the family doctor. Edgar could barely speak above a faint whisper. According to his doctor the strong medication had apparently damaged his throat. He did not speak for an entire year.

In March, 1901, with the help of the Squire and A. C. Layne, an acquaintance who was studying suggestive therapeutics and osteopathy, Edgar stretched out on the family couch and put himself to sleep just as he'd done with his spelling lesson. A few minutes later, when he had reached a deep sleep, Layne gave him instructions to look at his own body and describe the trouble in the throat, and how it could be corrected. When Edgar wakened, he coughed, spat a wad of blood, and spoke normally.

Layne and the Squire were jubilant. They predicted that if he could see his own body while he was asleep and identify both the problem and the solution, he could do the same thing for other people as well. Layne eagerly volunteered to be the guinea pig for an experimental reading. He pointed out that he heard there is a record in a person's mind of everything that goes on in his or her own body. He wanted to know if that was true.

Edgar thought the experiment sounded crazy, but out of gratitude for his own healing he was willing to try, reasoning that if he had the power to help himself it wouldn't be wrong to use it to help someone else.

The next day, with both Layne and the Squire present, he put himself to sleep so Layne could ask questions about his own poor physical condition. When Edgar woke, Layne was waving a well-scribbled notepad, and gleefully told him the perfect diagnosis had been given, complete with medicines, a diet, and exercises to correct his chronic stomach problem.

Edgar, who joked that he was the dumbest man in Christian County when he was awake, was stunned; bewildered. The names of the medicines Layne had written on his note pad were quite unfamiliar to him. He had never worked in a drugstore, or studied physiology, or biology, or chemistry, or anatomy. He knew nothing about such things, nor did he want to know.

Edgar was a devout Christian, a respected Sunday school teacher, and a life-long member of his church. All he ever wanted to do with his life, he said, was to be an ordained minister and follow the teachings of Jesus Christ as set forth in the Bible. Talking in his sleep was not what he had in mind.

The Squire told his son there was nothing wrong with having strange powers so long as they were used in God's work, and to remember that Jesus didn't pick His apostles from university professors, He chose simple fishermen.

Even so, when Edgar expressed fears that he might be accused of impersonating a medical doctor prescribing drugs, Layne explained that some of the preparations given through his reading were patent medicines, and others were simple mixtures that didn't require a prescription. He told Edgar he would soon know if they worked, because he intended to follow the instructions given in the reading to the letter.

A week later Layne, who was very much improved, encouraged Edgar to experiment with someone else. It was with a sense of trepidation that Edgar reluctantly agreed, but with the stipulation that he not be told who the person was, either before or after the experiment.

When Edgar opened his eyes, Layne was smiling from ear to ear, waving a pad filled with notes. According to him, it was another perfect diagnosis; exactly what a medical doctor had said months before. However, the doctor confided to the patient that the problem had no cure, at least not one that he knew of. Edgar's diagnosis, on the other hand, was reinforced with explicit directions to precipitate the perfect cure.

From the beginning it was clear that there was a difference between the aim of the readings and the aim of the average medical doctor. The doctor aimed at treating a specific aliment. The readings aimed at producing a healthy body which would eliminate the ailment itself.

Between that day and the time of his death on January 3, 1945, at the age of 67, Edgar Cayce gave more than 30,000 readings to save, or enrich, the lives of people; readings which are housed at the Association for Research and Enlightenment (A.R.E.) in Virginia Beach, Virginia. Obviously it was not meant for Edgar Cayce to help only a select few. His was a gift of God destined to benefit everyone.

Edgar was treated as a curiosity when word of his remarkable talent spread. On October 9, 1910, a full page display in the New York Times read, "Illiterate Man Becomes a Doctor When Hypnotized… Strange Power Shown by Edgar Cayce."

In response to the newspaper headline, Dr. Munsterberg, a German doctor from the Harvard School of Medicine, immediately went to Hopkinsville for the sole purpose of proving Edgar to be a simpleton and a fraud. That was before the pompous doctor watched in amazement as Edgar came into the room, removed his coat, loosened his necktie and shoelaces, laid on a long sofa, and went to sleep. A few minutes later the Squire spoke to him, telling him to have before him the body of a child living at such and such an address, to examine her and tell what was wrong with her body.

As soon as Edgar located the patient at her home in another state, he let out a long, deep sigh and went to work. A stenographer sat nearby to take down every word he said, and when he was done, she transcribed her notes, kept a copy, gave a copy to Dr. Munsterberg, and sent a copy to the patient's parents.

Dr. Munsterberg grudgingly went back to Harvard shaking his head. He found nothing wrong, or illegal, to expose in Hopkinsville;

only a modest, unpretentious man dedicated to helping others apparently by quoting from a universal mind.

Throughout the years Edgar Cayce was thoroughly investigated and unmercifully harassed by numerous medical doctors determined to prove he was a fraud. None was successful.

In November, 1931, when Edgar, his wife and his secretary were in New York on business, he was arrested on the spuriously devised charges of being a fortuneteller. After Magistrate Francis I. Erwin heard the testimony, he quickly dismissed the charges, saying they were frivolous.

Four years later, In December, 1935, Edgar Cayce was arrested and brought before a judge on charges of practicing medicine without a license. But, alas, it turned out to be just another bogus scheme contrived to protect the medical monopoly which produced nothing but the judge's rankled ire!

Edgar and Gertrude Cayce, along with their two sons, left their beloved Kentucky and moved to Virginia Beach, Virginia, where Edgar established his Association for Research and Enlightenment Foundation, and built a hospital to incorporate all manner of medical and alternative treatments to accommodate the various instructions given to people via the readings.

Even today, long after his death, the continuing popularity of Edgar Cayce's legend lives on as thousands of people from around the world visit the A.R.E. in Virginia Beach every year to study and decipher the readings.

*****

William Edward Gray, Bill to his family and friends, was another of God's special messengers.

Bill recharged and revitalized the human magnetic field, or master brain, to distribute energy to all parts and functions of the body. He had no medical diploma, but maintained that each of us comes into life with different talents which we develop to a greater or lesser degree. A talent like Bill's is special; not open to everyone.

Born in St. Paul, Minnesota, on July 13, 1895, Bill was *different* from his very first breath.

Before he could talk, he was receiving information from what he later called "the Powers," which, to him, was as natural as breathing. When he was little more than a toddler, Bill told his uncle to take Epsom salts to cure a severe case of dysentery. The uncle thought the kid was crazy, but Bill's mother advised him to do what the child said because, she whispered, he has ways we don't understand. The uncle reluctantly took the mixture young Bill handed him, and the next morning reported that all traces of the dysentery had disappeared.

Bill was only three or four years old when the family doctor, an older gentleman who made house calls by horse and buggy, recognized his special healing talent. He promised the little guy he could drive the team if he would go along and help with the patients. Bill became the doctor's constant companion.

At the age of six Bill declared his emancipation by telling his mother he had his own life to live. He didn't expect it would be easy he said, but he would not tolerate any interference with it along the way. And that was that!

Bill didn't play with other children. He preferred being alone. Setting out by himself in his sixth summer, he would be gone from home for days at a time tramping through the woods, sleeping under the stars, studying and learning from nature.

255

The fall after his sixth birthday Bill started to school, but the routine bored him and he quickly lost interest. Arithmetic and history came easy, but reading and spelling were impossible. Even as an adult he was a poor reader, although if he skimmed the first two or three pages, he instinctively knew what the whole book was about.

Bill quit school after fourth grade because he was certain that wisdom could be severely distorted by education. When he was fourteen he left home to face life as an adult, and found a job as a machinist's apprentice paying ten cents an hour for a ten-hour day. He learned quickly, and by his third day on the job could turn a shafting to different sizes on a lathe.

The International Harvester Company stole him away from his first employer. When he was twenty-one he became night foreman of the machine shop at Armour & Company, and later took a job as a machinist repairing stokers on the Great Northern Railroad.

Bill was restless. When he decided it was time to leave St. Paul, he became a traveling salesman because he wanted to travel and see other places; the whole United States, in fact.

In the spring of 1926, he bought a Willys automobile which he converted into a camper by making a few adjustments. He built in a pantry and icebox, and made frames covered with mosquito netting for the windows. His new rig allowed him to call on business accounts in four or five small towns every day, find a place to park at a nearby lake or stream at the end of business hours, and still have time to go fishing before dark.

He made a living by selling various products. He traveled, he fished, he studied nature in every state in the union; but most importantly, he healed hundreds of people along the way.

Through his strange talent, Bill used the powerful energy to rebuild the nervous system, relieve the pressures and tensions, and correct ailments by energizing a person's magnetic field naturally, because as he said, the human body was not created to utilize mechanically generated electrical currents. He accomplished this by placing his fingers over nerves, or nerve relay centers, in the lower abdomen and sending a blast of energy into the body through his hands to correct their physical problems. To him it was as natural as switching a radio dial from one wavelength to another.

In the fall of 1927, a letter forwarded by his mother caught up with him. It read, 'Come out and see what is wrong with my business.' It was signed, C. Hill, M.D. Bill, who was in Los Angeles at the time, headed to the San Francisco Bay area almost immediately to rendezvous with Dr. Hill.

The two men hit it off at first handshake. In the course of their getting acquainted conversation, Dr. Hill was summoned to the operating room, and on an impulse he asked Bill to tag along to watch him operate on a woman with a large abdominal cyst.

During the operation Bill watched Dr. Hill tighten his arm and manipulate his elbow on her chest in the heart area. Impulsively, he asked Dr. Hill if he was trying to give her energy.

Glancing up, the doctor yelled that if he knew anything at all about transferring energy he'd better get busy, and be quick about it.

Bill instantly put his hand on the left side of her abdomen beneath the sheet, and sent a charge of energy surging through her body. Immediately her shallow breathing became normal.

Back in the office, Dr. Hill looked silently at Bill for a time before congratulating him on the best display of moving vital energy through someone's body he'd ever seen. Thereafter, as Dr. Hill's special assistant, Bill frequently revitalized the magnetic fields of his patients.

In response to Dr. Hill's questions about his technique, Bill explained that he laid his ear to the patient's chest to get a "signal." As he listened, the body's vibrations revealed the location of tensions and nerve centers in spasm.

He said that by placing his fingers on certain areas of the body he generated a blast of energy to the troubled area that blended with the individual's own vital energy, and the correction was usually completed within a matter of minutes.

He went on to say that we accept, without argument, the influence of the moon on the tides because scientists tell us it is true. We do not dispute the revolving planets and changing seasons in relation to the sun. We have no reason to doubt that a magnetic electrical field governs planetary action. Why, then, is it so strange that a magnetic electrical field might govern human action as well? We are composed of innumerable atoms, and scientists report that the atom with its electrons has the same pattern as the sun and planets in a solar system; the same pattern that is in each cell in the human body.

Because of his many years of training in electronics and machinery, Bill viewed the body as an intricate machine which could function perfectly only with proper tuning, oiling, and energy. The life-force is that of electrical energy, he explained, and our bodies were constructed to conduct and transmit the human energy current.

He described the human body as the most sophisticated of all impulse relay machinery, and explained how it functions by combining systems similar to the automatic dial telephone, the computer, and other electronic devices. Each separate part of the body has its own intelligence which functions on human ray-energy, he said, not on standard electrical energy. The body will only utilize and retain human-ray energy. Man hasn't scratched the surface of this subject yet.

Why doesn't everyone know about this revolutionary new method of treating physical disorders? Bill was asked.

Revolutionary? New? Hardly!

He explained that the theory is as old as the world, even though, generally speaking, it's a lost art. The Bible records that some people in ancient days, and some in the New Testament, had the understanding and wisdom of healing through the laying on of hands. The same power passing through his hands, he said, resides in everyone, but not everyone has the knowledge of its application. He went on to say the Power does all the work. He merely acted as the distributor.

Dr. Hill and Bill Gray formed a partnership to subdivide land which Dr. Hill owned on the California side of Lake Tahoe. Thus, Bill became a very successful real estate salesman in 1930, at the height of the great depression. Sandwiched in between writing sales contracts, he treated scores of people; free, as usual.

In the summer of 1941, Bill decided to establish residence in Reno, Nevada. A lawyer in town told him that in order to establish legal residence it would be necessary to have a Nevada resident attest to the fact that he had been seen there at least once every twenty-four hours for six weeks. Bill checked into the Golden Hotel, a local landmark, and appointed one of the bellboys as his witness.

During the six weeks waiting period he treated all manner of human ailments. One morning a bellboy took him to the basement where he found the hotel engineer laying on the floor writhing in pain. Bill sent a charge of energy through the man and almost

259

immediately he was on his feet. One of the hotel managers asked Bill if he could do anything for his heart condition, which prevented him from working more than an hour or two a day. After a blast of Bill's magical energy the man was able to return to work fulltime.

A prominent local medical doctor sought Bill out, asking what he could do for his stroke paralysis. The doctor dragged one leg, walked with a crutch and a cane, and was unable to lift one arm. Immediately after receiving the charge the old doctor began swinging his arm over his head and kicking with his bad leg. News of his miraculous healing traveled fast when bystanders watched him walk out of the hotel carrying the crutch and swinging his cane.

The next morning a woman on two crutches found Bill in the hotel lobby, as did a state senator suffering crippling arthritis. Yesterday's healed medical doctor brought one of his worst heart patients after dinner that evening, and to settle a wager, took out his pocket watch to see how long it would take Bill to correct the problem. Two-and-a-half minutes.

The district attorney sent for Bill. He wanted to know how much money he had made from his healing work, and was surprised to learn that Bill had never charged, nor accepted money, for his services. Winking, Bill asked the district attorney why he didn't give him a letter saying he was not allowed to help people in Reno, so he could get some rest.

The district attorney scoffed at the suggestion, because, he said, he had orders from the governor of Nevada to get Bill licensed without delay. He was needed there.

The chairman of the board of supervisors in San Francisco came to Reno suffering from arthritis and a heart condition, and after a miraculous cure, he urged Bill to open an office in San Francisco.

When Bill arrived in San Francisco the chairman of the board of supervisors introduced him to the head of the city's health department, where a license for magnetic treatments was promptly issued.

A few weeks after Bill opened his office in San Francisco an official of the Mare Island Naval Shipyard near Vallejo said they desperately needed him in Vallejo because with World War II going on it was vitally important to keep employees on the job. Bill agreed to share his time between San Francisco and Vallejo for the next ten weeks. When one of his patients offered him a room in her big old house in Vallejo to use as his office, he graciously accepted.

Ten weeks came and went. Bill was still in Vallejo part time when, one day just as he was preparing to leave, a tall, thin man came in asking for Dr. Gray. Without responding, Bill ushered the man into his office. The stranger opened the conversation by saying he had a bad heart along with severe sinus and shoulder pain. When Bill put his ear to the man's chest he found no sign of either problem. However, he did find the man was filled with emotional tension caused by coming there under false pretense to cause trouble. Bill gave the guy a substantial charge of energy in his ribs…just to remember him by…which momentarily knocked him out. When he regained his composure the man got up and left without saying a word.

The next afternoon, Tuesday, July 11, 1944, the same man, who identified himself as Joseph Williams, Special Agent with the California State Board of Medical Examiners, along with a Vallejo police inspector, barged into Bill's office waving an arrest warrant. With the fury of a wild man, Williams ripped to shreds a pillow Bill had been sitting on, and turned all the chairs upside down looking for hidden electrical wires that he suspected had given him such a jolt the day before. The police inspector stood by, mystified and visibly embarrassed.

At the police station William Edward Gray was formally charged with treating the sick and afflicted without a state medical license. He posted a $500.00 cash bond before going back to his office to take care of a waiting room full of sick people, secure in his belief that he would be exonerated.

His trial lasted two full days, September 20 and 21, 1944, and according to the *TIMES HERALD*, Vallejo's daily newspaper, it was a humdinger! Due to the huge spirited crowd of people trying to elbow their way into the courtroom, the trial had to be moved to larger quarters.

The attorney general sent his ace deputy, who was medically trained, to prosecute the case, assisted by the local district attorney. Their first witness was the man on whom Bill had been working when he was arrested. The witness testified that before he came to Bill Gray his legs and arms were partially paralyzed and he could barely move them. The prosecutor wasn't interested in the man's physical condition. He only wanted to know how much he had paid for a series of treatments.

"About two-hundred dollars," the witness stated.

During cross examination, when Bill's attorney asked the witness to tell the court where he had been treated for that same condition before he found Bill Gray, he responded, "The Mayo Clinic, the Stanford University Hospital, the University of California Hospital, various other hospitals throughout the country, and I also saw several private medical specialists."

"Did you get much help from those previous treatments?" the defense attorney asked.

"No, sir, not a bit of help. I paid them thousands of dollars for nothing."

"When Mr. Gray generated energy to you, did you get any help?"

"I got immediate relief, paid him five dollars, and went back to work running my business."

And so it went throughout the trial.

When the prosecution's star witness, Joseph Williams, took the stand, the district attorney asked, "Did you feel any sensation of current or vibration from Mr. Gray's fingers?"

"I felt such a vibration as you might feel from the contracting of the muscles, nothing more."

The attorney placed his own fingers against the back of Williams' neck. "Do you feel any sensation now?"

"It doesn't feel a bit different from Gray's hands," he lied.

An entirely opposite picture was given by the seven women and one man called to the witness stand by the defense attorneys, who testified that Bill Gray had worked miracles by ridding them of everything from diabetes to blindness.

On the second day of the trial thirty additional witnesses testified for Bill Gray, mostly prominent civic leaders in San Francisco and Vallejo.

In his closing statement the defense attorney called the jury's attention to the fact that throughout history scientific men had scoffed at such things as the healing waters of Lourdes and other demonstrations of power which they could not understand. He pointed out that Mr. Gray had been subjected to that same kind of persecution at the hands of the medical profession.

The case went to a jury of twelve women who took less than twenty minutes to reach a verdict of **Not Guilty!**

Before Bill Gray retired in 1972 at the age of 77, he passed his knowledge and technique to a protégée, Dena L. Smith, M.D. Together, they healed thousands of people, and founded Life Energies Research Foundation in Burbank, California, to make his methods available to all who come seeking help in the future.

*****

Dr. Carey Reams, an ordained minister with a degree in Theology, a Ph.D. in Biochemistry, a Ph.D. in Biophysics, was a man far ahead of his time.

Born in Orlando, Florida in 1904, Carey Reams was an unusually bright, curious little boy who enjoyed a happy, somewhat normal early childhood.

His life's work actually began when he was five years old. A circuit rider preached one Sunday a month at the church his family attended, and, as was the custom, after church he relished a good meal at the table of one of the parish families.

Entering into dinner table conversation one Sunday, young Carey told Brother Smith that he didn't believe anything he said in his sermon that day; a sermon which was about the resurrection of the dead, and how, when Jesus comes the graves would be opened and the people would get up and go to meet Him. (Thessalonians 4:13-18)

In response to Brother Smith's chuckle, asking what he didn't understand, Carey looked directly at him and asked if he didn't know that when something dies it goes to dust and cannot be put back together again?

Brother Smith tried to explain that when he grew older he would understand such things, but in fact, the older Carey became

264

the less he understood. The more he thought about it, the more perplexed he became.

He studied chemistry in high school and college in pursuit of the answer. Complicated chemical formulas guided him to complex mathematical equations which immediately piqued his interest. Carey Reams soon became known among his peers as an Einsteinian mathematical genius.

He seriously considered becoming a medical doctor in those days. However, finances and medical school quotas made that dream impossible, so he shifted his emphasis to the study of diet and nutrition. As part of the curriculum, he learned to analyze fruits, orange juice, tomatoes, carrots, beans, and other fruits and vegetables grown locally in Florida.

A carrot was not always a carrot, he discovered, because some of them contained up to 300-milligrams of iodine per gram, while others contained only 2-parts of iodine per gram. But why? Why?

His experiments encouraged him to study dietetics, but he became very discouraged when the teachers' only approach to diet was to count calories. Calorie counting was not the answer he was looking for. His curious mind demanded to know the exact amount of nutrition an individual could expect from each food eaten.

Not finding the answers he was looking for in dietetics as the subject was taught in those days, Carey transferred to an agricultural college to study the biophysics of nutrition in various soils; a topic, he soon discovered, that'd had little, if any, previous investigation.

In Ag school he ran into a German physicist who taught that everything lives upon its own frequency...people, animals, plants; everything. For example, he explained, grapes have their own frequency, or molecular structure, and he shared the frequency

265

number for grapes with Carey. Having a mathematical equation for a specific food was awesome. Not only was it something he understood, he instinctively knew he was finally on the right track to finding an answer to the question he asked Brother Smith when he was five years old.

To earn extra money for college expenses, Dr. Reams established a medical laboratory; one of the first in the southeastern United States. One day the local police brought some ashes gleaned from a building destroyed in a recent fire to his laboratory and asked if he could identify them as those of a dog, a cat, or possibly a human.

After spending several days studying ashes he borrowed from a local undertaker's crematory where the gender was known, he discovered the frequency on which human beings live; log frequency 24 for the human male, log frequency 26 for the human female. It was a tremendously exciting discovery.

Dr. Reams very confidently reported to the police that the ashes were the remains of two human females and one human male. He was also able to identify their race. The police were astounded. His report verified the death of a woman and her two children whom they had suspected were in the building when it burned.

Based on this discovery, long hours, weeks, months, of extensive research proved that every living thing, according to its kind and sex, has a frequency like no other. Starting with the foundation number of 24 for man, and 26 for woman, and adding the numbers of tiny microscopic cells in the blood of lymph known as the microphage, the millimicrophage, and the milli-millimicrophage, which are always different, he could develop a specific individual number for each and every person ever born. As it says in the song, **when your number is called up yonder....**

At last, some thirty years after he asked Brother Smith how God could put us together again, he could prove the answer was in the numbers.

One afternoon a neighbor asked Dr. Reams to look at his three-year-old son who had been diagnosed as an epileptic by medical doctors. Because he experienced up to eight seizures a day, the child had a life expectancy of only five years, they said. Medical science had exhausted its resources. The father pleaded for help.

Even though he didn't know quite where to begin Dr. Reams went to work on the problem, firm in his belief that there was no such thing as an incurable disease. If only he knew the child's perfect number, he reasoned, he could create a diet that would bring his body chemistry back to its perfect number. Taking that theory one step further, he knew disease and illness could not exist in a body with a perfect number.

In answer to his fervent prayers, he was guided to test the boy's urine and saliva. Thus, he came up with a mathematical equation of what his perfect body chemistry should be. The test results indicated the child was actually experiencing low blood sugar dips which caused, or resembled, seizures. Creating a diet to restore his body to its perfect pH number, based on the numbers in various plants, was easy. A diet to restore, or maintain, perfect pH balance is definitely an individual thing. One size (one diet) does not fit all.

After three months on the diet Dr. Reams created for him, the boy was free of all seizures. When he ran into Dr. Reams thirty-five years later he reported that he was married, had two healthy children, and had never had another seizure.

A tragic accident significantly altered this passionate mission that was to become Carey Ream's life work. In his late thirties when World War II began, he enlisted in the United States Army as an officer, and acting as a chemical engineer, was assigned to the Special Operations Forces in the Philippines.

Only a few days after he arrived in Luzon in 1945, a truck in which he was riding was blown to smithereens when it hit a land mine. Even though Reams miraculously lived, he returned home a quadriplegic. Five years later, close to death, his condition worsening by the day, he insisted on being taken to Philadelphia to attend a Katherine Kuhlman faith healing service.

With the help of Ms. Kuhlman, and a profound life-altering spiritual experience he had that night, he walked out of the auditorium unaided. Soon thereafter he enrolled in divinity school, and after graduation, became an ordained minister, an accomplishment that played a major role in his future life's work; work that was not only holistic in nature, but also Divinely guided.

Dr. Carey Reams was a brilliant agronomist. His mantra: We don't live off the food that we eat; **we live off the energy contained in the food we eat!** We live from the **life** in what we consume. The body needs raw, living, nutrient-dense fruits and vegetables every day. Asparagus and celery contain natural arsenic, which strengthens the heart muscle. Green vegetable juices strengthen the pancreas. A wide variety of fruits and vegetables supply most of the minerals the body must have in order to function properly. Refined products such as white sugar and white flour deplete minerals from the body and leave energy reserves low. The body must have sufficient minerals.

Dr. Reams worked diligently to develop what he called the **biological theory of ionization.** The process of ionization is the law of putting things together and taking them part, ion by ion.

In his ongoing quest to learn the definitive number of each plant, and how energy is created from the food we eat, he made some startling discoveries when he tested meats, and fresh fruits and vegetables, to determine exactly what it was that human nutrition required.

Seven years of stoically focused research led him back to the laws of food in the Old Testament. (Leviticus: 11, Deuteronomy: 14) The following should not be included in the human diet: hogs, guinea pigs, rabbits, catfish, tuna fish, lobsters, oysters, clams, shrimp, crabs, scallops, and shell fish of any kind.

These foods, he found, release energy too quickly for the body to assimilate. They digest much too fast for the body to utilize the proteins, which turn into urea and enter the blood stream so fast the kidneys cannot eliminate them. Sooner or later, a urea build-up leads to serious health problems.

Dr. Reams, a highly respected, much sought after agronomist, traveled extensively teaching farmers how to grow exceptionally high-yield, nutrient-dense crops free of disease and pests. His travels provided an opportunity for about one-hundred people a year from all over the country to seek him out for personal help. Among them was a young woman dying of Hodgkin's disease. Her mother brought her to Dr. Reams after medical doctors predicted she would die in less than thirty days.

After testing her urine and saliva, the diet Dr. Reams developed to rebalance her body pH immediately set her on the road to recovery. Because she was so grateful to be alive, she included a note in her Christmas cards that year to share the good news with family and friends.

Before he got out of bed early on a cold, frosty January morning a couple of weeks after Christmas, vehicles filled with sick people were lined up in his driveway, and for three blocks down the street. Dr. Carey Reams and his unusual talent had suddenly been discovered, thanks to a grateful young woman who once had Hodgkin's disease.

When the workload became too demanding with people knocking on his door at all hours, Dr. Reams and his wife found a quiet, peaceful, forty-four acre hideaway nestled in the Blue Ridge Mountains in Georgia, up a long winding dirt road with confusing forks and no directional signs, far beyond the nearest paved road. The real estate agent swore nobody would find them there.

Even so, during the next few years Dr. Reams tested, and tailored individual diets for about twelve-thousand people from all over the world who, without an address or directions, found his retreat. More than half of them had received a death notice from their medical doctors. Only five of those diagnosed terminal failed to respond to diet.

No medical doctor, no hospital, could match his record. They did not have instruments to compete with his simple urine/saliva test that could detect conditions such as calcium and mineral deficiencies; high/low/normal blood sugar; candida yeast, or parasites; circulatory and heart problems; high/low blood pressure; arthritis; weight gains; high cholesterol; nor did they have the wherewithal to eliminate any of them from the body.

To retaliate against his outstanding success in saving lives, the American Medical Association filed a lawsuit against Dr. Carey Reams in May, 1970, accusing him of practicing medicine without a license. He was yanked out of his bed at two o'clock in the morning, and hauled off to jail where he was kept for nine hours before he was permitted to post bail.

The American Medical Association filed the same charges against him in April, 1972, and again in February, 1976, and in May, 1976.

Dr. Reams told the court that he was not against medical doctors. He did not practice medicine, he said, nor did he tell people not to take medicine. As an ordained minister, he simply taught the health message as written in the Bible.

The case went all the way to the Georgia Supreme Court, where Dr. Reams confidently backed up his claims with indisputable scientific mathematical data and formulas.

Apparently because the American Medical Association viewed Dr. Reams as a monumental threat to their status quo, an uncontrollable maverick who could run mental circles around their doctors and scientists, they hounded him night and day, accusing him of one little picayune thing, then another.

Dr. Carey Reams, a quiet, humble man sent by God to shine a brilliant new light to illumine the path of those seeking happy, disease-free lives, had endured quite enough of their harassment. He and his wife abruptly moved to England where he fulfilled the academic requirements, got the piece of parchment he needed to get the American Medical Association out of his life, and took his new medical license back to the United States ready to legally pick up his work where he left off.

Instead of solving the problem, the situation worsened when Dr. Reams refused to join the American Medical Association. Because, as a non-member, they could not control him or take credit for his brilliant discoveries, they made his life a living hell.

Dr. Carey Reams was an honest Christian man with high morals and impeccable ethics which made it impossible to practice medicine according to the A.M.A.'s dictate, since he was fully dedicated to pH balancing the soil, and treating people holistically through diet, nutrition and herbs. He sincerely believed, and taught, that ingesting any kind of drugs, and/or chemicals, would prove to be highly detrimental to the human body. He never wavered from that belief.

Dr. Reams was dogged throughout the rest of his life by the medical authorities who objected to his use of nutritional healing and nutrition-based preventative medicine. Instead of caving in to their whims, he opened several holistic clinics across the United States to teach people about his methods and how they could test themselves to find their own perfect numbers.

If people understand the principles he discovered and appropriately apply them, they can, indeed, enjoy a long, healthy life, because whatever the age, the numbers will be the same as those in his perfect health equation. The validity of his nutrition-enhanced vitality was demonstrated in his own life when he re-married and fathered a child when he was eighty years old.

Dr. Reams continued to teach agriculture and human health classes until his death in the late 1980s. His valiant contribution to humanity is still being taught in the United States and, in fact, is even more important today than ever before.

His was a message that will live forever!

Tips and comments by Dr. Reams:

- There is no such thing as an incurable disease.
- Anger and fear are the body's greatest enemies.
- Most disease, including cancer, is caused by a lack of minerals in the body.
- Chemotherapy damages the liver. A person many not die of cancer, but they will die of a liver problem.
- The reason doctors have not found a cure for cancer; they're looking in the wrong place.

- Americans do not drink enough water. Drink only distilled water. The juice of three fresh lemons in a gallon of distilled water is good for proper pH balance.
- There is less damage to the body by drinking a good freshly brewed coffee than in drinking decaffeinated coffee.
- From a Biblical standpoint, nutrition and natural therapy should be the first mode of treatment, not the last.
- Most people go the medical route first, then when they are broken physically, they turn to alternative treatment…sometimes too late.
- Children under 12 years of age should not have meat of any kind.
- Children under 8 years of age should not eat nuts, or nut butters.

*****

And now comes Solomon J. Wickey to deliver the most profound message of all: **tap into God's power to heal by sending a coded signal to the body via silent thought.**

The practice will be the way of the future, and Solomon is not the only one who recognizes that probability. In an interview for the January, 2000, issue of Prevention Magazine, Andrew Weil, M.D. pointed out that there is nothing new about energy medicine. There are those who have been tapping into energy's power to heal for decades, but it's the subtler, less understood, less measurable forms of energy healing that will factor into medicine's future, including energies found in ancient healing traditions, or those produced by energy healers.

If this sounds a bit farfetched, or "woo-woo," think of energy healing as simply harnessing the power of an invisible force.

A dedicated scientific exploration of energy medicine might reveal how homeopathy and other holistic therapies work, and once understood, could possibly expand their healing powers to add very potent weapons to medicinal arsenals, because unlike the powerful chemicals currently being used against diseases such as cancer, energy techniques historically have few, if any, side effects.

Dr. Weil confided that in his opinion, we can expect energy medicine to come into its own in the next few years.

*****

Through His special messengers God is apparently trying to convince mankind that modern day medicine, including surgery and prescription drugs, has a significant place in the scheme of human health, but makes up a very small percentage of the overall equation, a percentage that is steadily shrinking as people seek out options that provide more desirable results. Instead of trying to interfere with God's plan, medical doctors might be well advised to learn about, and implement, these new techniques, because their efforts to destroy His messages to mankind will never be successful.

The thought of excellent life-long health free from pain, debilitating side effects, expensive insurance premiums, or government control and/or intervention, is exciting to people willing to take charge of their own lives.

Dr. Carey Reams and Solomon J. Wickey shared their respective messages and techniques with hundreds of students who, in turn, will one day share them with the masses until they become commonplace.

Perhaps the release codes are only the beginning. Could it be possible that the next plateau will be the development of an individual code for each person; a simple code they can use to correct all of their own body's malfunctions upon command? The mere possibility deserves serious, judicious contemplation.

Solomon Wickey is, and will long be remembered as, one of the greatest men of our time. This humble, gentle man has unwaveringly clung to his convictions in spite of the many obstacles placed in his path. His reputation has been defiled, his character assassinated and vilified. He has been made fun of, tormented, shunned and excommunicated by egotistical power-driven men who would have their charges believe they are true men of God. A public apology by those responsible is in order, lest someone with the attitude of Big Fist or the Green Beret at the trial in 1983 decides to pay a visit.

The dedication and courageous perseverance he consistently demonstrated throughout his life has made it possible for untold thousands of people to be generously blessed by God through nothing more than Solomon's Touch.

**We have no credentials,
except that He chose us.**

D. K. Jones

Bibliography:

Edgar Cayce: **There Is A River**, by Thomas Sugure. Sugure personally interviewed Cayce for this book.
William Edward Gray: **Born To Heal**, by Ruth Montgomery; the **Vallejo Times Herald.**
Dr. Carey Reams: **Acres, USA; Health Guide for Survival,** by Salem Kirban. For more information, check the Internet.

TESTIMONIAL LETTERS

BILLY DAVID ANDERSON

December 30, 2003

Dear Mr. Solomon Wickey:

Mr. Wickey words cannot express the thanks that we send to you from our hearts for sharing your healing gift with our son, Joshua. We visited with you in the beginning of October after our son spending near 1 1/2 years in absolute pain with Chrone's Disease. After leaving your office he has not had one pain or symptom, he is like a regular 18 year old boy now. his recovery is nothing short of a miracle sent as a blessing from our Heavenly Father through your hands. Thank you for being a vessel through which this gift can be shared our family has been blessed in more ways than one through your loving example of selfless sharing.

Please find enclosed a small expression of my personal gratitude. This pen and ink drawing is presented to you in the same loving charitable manner in which you share your gift.

With deepest sincere thanks:

Dave Anderson

I first went to Solomon because I had migraine headaches. I'd suffered with them since I was eight, and the older I got the worse they became. I had been to several doctors, specialists and hospitals. The last specialist I went to put me on two different kinds of preventives and all the pain medicine I wanted. It still didn't help. I didn't like being drugged up.

The headaches were so bad I was in bed from two to seven days a week. I felt useless and worthless to my family. I didn't want to be here anymore.

A friend told me about Solomon and my husband took me to see him. My head hurt when we got there, and after a long wait, we finally got in to see this Amish man who helps people.

Looking at him I thought, "This man is going to touch me and I'm going to get better...yeah, right!" But as soon as I sat in front of him a tremendous calming feeling came over me.

When he asked what my problem was, I told him I had excruciating headaches.

"Some worse than others?" he asked.

I said, "Yes."

After a quick test, he gently touched my knee, then my abdomen, and smiled as he said the problem would be completely gone in about two weeks.

My headache eased up instantly.

When I asked him what I owed him, he said, "Nothing."

I said, "Thank you!"

He said, "Don't thank me, thank God."

I did, and still do.

Solomon gave me my life back, and I wanted to do something for him. I was raising registered Paint horses at the time, and had a beautiful black and white colt which I offered to him. He said he would buy it, but I said no, I wanted to give it to him for helping me and my family, and so many others. Finally, he agreed to accept the colt.

That was five years ago, and I haven't had a migraine since.

Judy Kennett

August 7, 1977 took our lives in another direction.

Dick was operated on for Klatskins Tumor, which attacks the bile ducts. It is a very aggressive cancerous tumor. When the surgeon operated he thought he would be able to save the liver, but found that he could not, so he removed the gall bladder and closed him up. He came out and told us "get your affairs in order, he has six months to live."

I couldn't believe what I had heard. Our lives had never been so out of control. We were like fish out of water. We prayed a lot, and God showed us the way through our friends, Walt and Margerite. They introduced us to Solomon Wickey. With God's help, he gave us hope.

Solomon put Dick on the cancer diet, told us that if we didn't cheat, there was light at the end of the tunnel for Dick.

We continued to see the oncologist, just to monitor Dick's progress, but Dick refused chemo and radiation and did not tell them about Solomon because they don't believe. We weren't going to spend time trying to defend Solomon's way. After two-and-a-half months the medical doctors couldn't understand where the cancer had gone.

Finally they turned us loose, saying they weren't doing anything for us. Dick assured them they were, because they were because they were confirming the fact that the cancer was gone.

It has been 7 years! Even though our telephone is unlisted, people seem to find us and come to us asking for help. We take them to see Solomon, our wonderful gifted man of God.

Forever thankful,

Dick and Jayne Rhodes

I love Solomon Wickey. His laughter and light heart are a huge part of my healing. I'm from Indiana but have been living in New York. Every trip back home, I write and ask to see him. He is my "doctor," and my teacher.

The first time I saw him, I had been diagnosed with Epstein bar, chronic fatigue, low blood pressure, low blood sugar, and pre-cancerous cells. This was overwhelming and left me distraught.

A friend reminded me of Wickey, so I went to Indiana, picked up my Mom in Indianapolis, and headed to his place near Madison on Sunday afternoon where I took a number out of a box (# 25) so I could return the next day. We were the 25th carload to see him.

He asked me what the trouble was. When I related what I had been told, he checked my eyes and some other things. He agreed that I had low blood sugar, and said my eyes indicated that I'd had it since childhood. I took licorice root and chromium for eight months.

On another visit my eyes showed a yeast infection. He told me a story about his cow while he worked on it, and when he was done, he sent me outside to look at his horses and rest for a while before driving.

I have many stories about my experiences with Solomon. I've taken people, and sent people to see him, but, personally, I always go to get a dose of good ole knee-slapping laughter, a glimpse at a simple world, and the opportunity to sit with someone I call a Master.

Solomon gave me my life. My blood sugar had always been so far off that I had never known what it was like to feel good. I'll never forget the day he said to me, "You are going to start feeling good....finally!" He totally understood what I'd been through.

So, like I said, I love Wickey. I'll see him as long as we're both alive. I am so grateful for this wonderful man. May God richly bless him!

With love,

Andrea
New York City

I was sick for many years with liver, kidney, stomach, and skin problems, as well as arthritis, even though I was only in my 30s. Prior to this, I learned about Solomon from working with many other holistic doctors.

I realized how special Solomon was right away. I could see how God was working through him.

One day I was so ill I could not walk. My back was filled with pain. I didn't have an appointment to see Solomon, but my husband drove me to his office in hopes that he would take a moment to see me.

When we got there the waiting room was filled with ailing people waiting to see him as well.

I remained in the car while my husband went to ask if there was some chance Solomon could see me. He graciously said he would to see me, and my husband carried me into his office past the room full of waiting people.

Solomon worked on me for what seemed like an extremely long time. The pain was almost unbearable. I was ringing wet with perspiration throughout my entire body.

When he finished, he left me rest and regain my composure for a few minutes, then he told me to get up and walk. I couldn't believe it....I could walk!!! I felt drained, but free of pain.

We left his office through the same crowded waiting room, and to my surprise, they all clapped as I walked by.

Solomon has been a gigantic influence in my life; especially his strong faith and spiritual strength. He taught me that **anything** is possible through faith and asking for God's help.

Nancy Niekamp
Minster, Ohio

Let me tell you how I met Solomon Wickey.

I felt really bad! My friend, Pat, said, "Dolly, I wish you would go with me to see Solomon. I know he can help you."

I wanted to go for a long time, but couldn't talk my husband into taking me. When we walked into his office, Solomon found a lot of gallstones when he looked in my eyes through the glass.

I asked him why the doctor didn't find them when they took a lot of ex-rays at the hospital. He said because they were hidden by all the plastic around them, and asked if I'd been eating oleo and margarine? I confessed that I had. He said, Dolly, eat butter. Butter is better for you.

I changed to butter immediately, and started feeling much better right away. My cholesterol came back down to normal, too.

Solomon is the best!

Dolly, from Ohio

May 21-04

Soloman

Words alone cannot
describe someone that
has done so much
for so many for no
more than a mere
Thank you.
Smartest man in
the World - an
ANGEL from God
are a few of the
names given Him.

Jack Vaughn
Guilford, In

We heard about Solomon and his healing gift from a business partner in the late 90's. Since my business partner had a great deal of creditability with us and had experienced Solomon's healing touch, we decided to visit him one day. In the fall of 2001 I felt the urge and need to visit Solomon and departed on a 16-hour trip from New Orleans to Auburn Indiana with my wife.

We decided to enter the visit with faith that God would use Solomon's touch to heal any ailment that we may have had. I will never forget our first visit as Solomon looked into my eyes for a moment with a flashlight and magnifying glass, he leaned back in his chair a giggled some. I was curious as of his demeanor and he stated that I had stress blockages and that they were released. Being a person of faith I immediately noticed the way he had articulated his sentence, "your blockages are released".

Since then my family and I have made 3-additional trips back to see Solomon for a variety of physical needs and have always received our healing. We personally have known over 40-people who he has helped with both physical and spiritual ailments. Needless to say during every visit we received everything expected. A gentle spirited man that cares more about people than anyone we have ever known; someone who selflessly gives of his time for the health and well being of people. We thank God through Jesus Christ for the anointing and healing power that he has gifted to him and honor Solomon for heeding the call and becoming the person God created him to be.

Tommy and Dana Vadell
Slidell Louisiana

Mr. Wickey has helped me so much. I could write a book!

It's been at least eight to ten years since I first met him. Actually, it was my husband who went, but I asked Solomon to check me, too, because I had really bad neck, shoulder and back pain.

The chiropractor I went to wanted me to see a surgeon, but after visiting Solomon, I was back to normal and turning my neck both ways without pain.

When I discovered a lump in my breast, the doctor sent me for a mammogram, and said it was cancer. I had a lumpectomy, but refused chemo and radiation even when the doctor said I was playing with fire if I didn't.

I went to see Solomon, and for the next four months followed his very strict cancer diet to the letter. That was April, 2002. Two years later, I am still cancer free, and continue to see Solomon, and also have regular mammograms.

Forty-five years ago I had Bells Palsey. I was pregnant with my fourth child and couldn't take anything to help. By the time I could do something about it, I already had some shrinkage of that facial nerve, so have had to live with it all this time. As I got older it bothered me more. I asked Solomon about it had learned he had already been working on it. Now I can't tell it was ever there. It was especially noticeable in a picture, but we had our 50th anniversary last year, and praise God, the picture was good!

I believe Solomon has a God given anointing, and I know God led me to him. I am so grateful!

Mary Evelyn Speer

I had a terrible pain in my back just below my left shoulder blade that worsened day by day. By the fourth or fifth day, the pain was almost unbearable, but I had an important appointment, so I struggled through it.

As I was driving home, all I could think about was going to see Solomon for help. Suddenly his release codes popped into my mind. Right there as I drove down the highway, I quickly tested on myself to see if I could find the problem. It was so exciting when I found stones in my kidneys, and eliminated them by using a release code. My body responded immediately, and before I turned into my driveway less than ten minutes later, the pain was gone, and it didn't come back, either.

What a blessing! I thank God every day for showing us this wonderful new technique through His servant, Solomon Wickey.

M.J.S.
Southern Indiana

Upon the onset of back aches and numbness in my right arm I consulted my physician. My physician said we would need to conduct a series of tests which would be a process of elimination to find the cause of the disorder.

I was sent for an MRI which showed in the x-rays three herniated discs in my upper cervical spine. I was immediately sent to a neurosurgeon who said surgery was the most common procedure to correct my injury. It would involve fusing two or more of my spinal discs together. He also said that if I did not want to have surgery right away I could go through a series of Physical Therapy appointments, or possible have a "nerve block" injection into the nerve to deaden the pain and subsequently ease the disorder temporarily. This would only delay the inevitable...surgery.

I decided that since I had visited Solomon Wickey for severe migraine headaches and he has been successful in eliminating them I would once again seek his help.

Solomon quickly found not three, but seven herniated discs and within minutes of his touch the pain began to ease and subsequently disappear. To this day I remain pain and numbness free. I cancelled my follow-up appointment with the neurosurgeon and have been able to function as normally as I did before the onset of the disc disorder.

Brett Anderson

I was near death over fifteen years ago at the age of thirty, when I first went to see Solomon Wickey. My family and I are sure that if it had not been for God working through Solomon, I wouldn't be alive today.

I always tell people who ask about Solomon, that after being in the room with him I always feel peaceful and uplifted. It gives me a feeling of what it would be like being in the presence of a prophet of God. The energy that I get from him is positive, peaceful and fulfilling.

I have spent many hours with Solomon over the years. Some were in tears, some in laughter, some filled with encouraging wisdom, a few were admonishing, and sometimes he needed encouragement from me.

I know one thing with all my heart….Solomon is truly a man of God, and is led by the Holy Spirit!

Connie Beer

Solomon is a precious soul to whom God has given the ability to help all humanity learn how to help themselves.

He has helped me grow spiritually and has taught me to how to help others. I'm sure he's responsible for saving my husband's life.

My husband was dying from colitis, and some emotional concerns. We used herbs and God's energy to help him heal his colon, and himself. Solomon helped me both physically and emotionally, through this difficult time.

My husband Tom's digestive system is much improved. He might have died if it had not been for this precious man.

I will always love Solomon!

C.H.
Minster, Ohio

I praise God for putting Solomon Wickey in my life to show me a whole new way of nutrition through herbs.

I had been using doctors and chiropractors two to three times a week, because of achiness, pain, soreness in my joints, and burning in the esophagus to the point that it was difficult to eat.

After an ultrasound, the doctor found "something" on my liver and sent me for a CAT scan and MRI. I had an MRI on a Sunday morning, and by Sunday evening the doctor called to say they still couldn't determine what it was, but he said exploratory surgery was needed.

I had gone to Solomon in Madison one time before that, but after knowing nothing but medicine all my life, I was very skeptical. But when I hung up the phone from the doctor, my husband said, "I'm taking you to the Amish man tomorrow." So we made the hour and a half trip and sat for several hours in Sol's front yard waiting to see him.

He told me there were no masses on my liver, but he found toxicity in my body caused from eating hydrogenated oils and other bad food and chemicals. Since that time, Solomon has helped me with numerous things that have occurred as a result of improper diet and chemicals.

I have so much respect, gratitude, appreciation and love for Solomon Wickey. He is such a generous, loving, obedient to the Lord man, who always makes you feel good when you see him. I know that I, my family, and my friends, have been truly blessed to have this special man with the healing touch in our lives.

C. Capan
Maineville, Ohio

Our thanks to Solomon

My husband and I wish to thank Solomon.

For me, I am a three year cancer survivor thanks to Solomon's diet.
Then there was a much smaller matter of the knuckles on the top of my
hands that I had just dug at for years and they were calloused and always
cracking open and bleeding. I just thought they were going to look bad
permanently, but thought I would ask Solomon if there was anything he
could do with these scarred hands. And sure enough the backs of my hands
look just as they did before the calluses.

My husband was just having his first check up with Solomon when Solomon
asked him when he had hurt his back, my husband was shocked as he had
forgotten about his back and had not mentioned it to anyone, as it had been
many years that they had told him he might have to have back surgery,
because they thought he had a bad disk. He told them that he would wait and
was in a brace for awhile and it all turned out ok.
He also had a problem with his elbow bothering him that he was unable to
pick up heavy things and it hurt just to move it, but no more thanks to
Solomon and his gift.

Solomon can tell so many things about our health and help cure what ails us.
It's so amazing and we're so grateful and ask for God's special blessings for
this very special man.

Sharon and Gordon of Harrison, Ohio

293

Many times Solomon has helped our family and the friends that I have brought to see him. The time I was most grateful was when my daughter had been injured in an accident when she was shopping. Shelving fell on her head, compressing her spine, damaging 4 vertebrae in her neck, breaking her nose and two ribs. She had been in a lot of pain for some time and was not getting better. Solomon was able to help her and start the healing process.

My training is as a Certified Natural Health Professional. When I can't figure out what is wrong, I turn to Solomon. He always has the remedy. Recently he was able to discover why my eyes would swell and itch several days a week. His suggestions worked and I am free of this terrible annoyance. My family has come from Missouri on more than one occasion to seek his help. He was able to give a solution when even Mayo Clinic couldn't help. Bless this wonderful healer!

Sincerely,

Marlene French

Marlene French, CNHP
Michigan

Solomon J. Wickey is a vessel for God and is used as such by God to help God's children. Solomon has helped me and others that I have sent and/or taken to visit him. I am sure he has saved my life and others! I have went to him on crutches and walked out carrying them under my arm and this has also happened to others that I know. God has allowed Solomon to see my and others many health problems, physical and mental, and had been either "released" and/or corrected with herbs and some life style changes. I had one relative that could not move his own wheel chair that he had been confined in and after seeing Solomon that relative walked out of Solomon's office under his own power, to the amazement of the people that was sitting in Solomon's office area for they had surely seen a breathing dead man being carried wheel chair and all into Solomon's office a few minutes before. The many miracles that has happened with the touch of Solomon, God's touch, are far too many to write down here. I once had asked Solomon how he does what he does and he answered by saying that "You can lie to me but your body can not lie to God"!!!

Kevin

Solomon is a special person
to us. He been there when I
have give up and he has a gift
from God. He has took care
of us for many years.

God Bless Him
Robert & Martha Wood

What a difficult, but wonderful, letter to write. Difficult, because how can I put all the miracles with which Mr. Wickey has blessed us into words?

My husband had back surgery about fifteen years ago. The surgery was not successful so he suffered with constant, almost unbearable pain. After all those years of therapy and chiropractic treatments up to twice a week he never got any relief. Another surgery seemed to be looming in his future.

After the first visit to Solomon Wickey his back was straight as an arrow, and completely pain free. That first visit was three and a half years ago.

My son has always suffered from boils; as many as three a month. After he saw Solomon, a horrible boil vanished overnight, and today he is still boil free.

As for me, I never had gallstone surgery because they suddenly vanished. I also broke my arm in three places and it was not healing. After Solomon's miracle touch, it healed quickly.

It is so hard to point out just a few of our blessings from Mr. Wickey, because there have been so many and they just keep coming.

I can only say that we thank God for having met Solomon Wickey, a man who is truly blessed by the hand of God.

Jeff and Marilyn Morgan

SOLOMON J. WICKEY

My life, people and animals of our world are much healthier for the dear soul, Solomon J. Wickey. I thank him and his family for the sacrifices made doing their work. I am also grateful that he is my herbalist, teacher and friend. I was blessed to be able to study with Solomon and be welcomed by him and his family. Our wonderful times, outings and meals will always be remembered.

God Bless You, Sir

Faye Russell
Monticello, KY

Dear Solomon,

The signature of God's love is written all over your life. Your wisdom has touched and inspired me on my own life's journey of educating others in health, philosophy, spirituality, and emotions.

With the knowledge I have gained by observing your gift of herbal mastery, my future has been set in motion. Thank you for sharing. Thank you for the memories...the most treasured is sitting by the stream at a picnic with your sons and you playing your harmonicas...such a quality of life has been an inspiration to me. Your family values, respect, and love for others is a signature of God ...written all over my life.

Jeanne Bergman

May 26, 2004

To whom it may concern:

When I heard a biography was being written about Solomon Wickey, I wanted to be able to participate. If I am too late for the book, I do hope that Sol will get a copy of this.

Over 20 years ago, as a young woman I fell ill and found no help from the medical profession. My in-laws heard about Sol who was helping so many people and asked if we would go if they'd take us. We had nothing to lose so why not? Uncle Obed Gerber made the appointment which for some reason happened to be on Sol's day off. When we got there, having driven 90 miles, Sol and Anna were at the grocery store and believe it or not, we went to town and found them just loading out their groceries in the buggy. He rode home in the car and proceeded to work on me. Is that Christ-like or what??????

Over a period of time, we went every other week, and he told us that it would take 6 months before we noticed any improvement and then at a year some more improvement and at 18 months slightly more improvement. He was right on! I followed whatever he told me to do and I found out you can get used to most any awful tasting stuff, even raw egg yolks in a shake which I drank many, many mornings.

Improvement was slow, and one had to almost drive stakes to see where you came from, but after 11 years of being on a very strict diet, with lots of vitamins and minerals and herbs as suggested by Sol, one day told me I could get off the diet that restricted me from wheat, oats, rye and barley grains. I have been doing so well since then and we give God thanks Who worked through Sol Wickey to heal me.

He is a godly man, who is very willing to be in the center of God's Will by serving others lovingly, unselfishly, and I'd like to say untiringly, but I know he tires. People have drained dear Sol of his energy at times and yet he still perseveres as he knows this is where God wants him to be at this time. Sol and Anna Wickey and family are loved and prayed for and esteemed highly by us.

Will and Sue Schieler

Milford, IN

Solomon has blessed our lives for many years by helping us with our countless health needs.

The biggest challenge for us came when my 12 year old son suddenly became severely ill with an unknown illness which left him in a wheelchair. Solomon was very helpful relieving his pain and sticking with us for the last 8 years to make his life the best it could be, and to guide him on the journey back to health.

We spent much time with doctors, hospitals, medical tests, and specialists out of state; none of which helped my son. When we met Solomon and his helpers, they were able to reduce his pain and make him strong enough to return to school and have a life again.

Solomon is truly blessed by God and shares that gift freely with all of us. My family is very thankful to know him and to benefit from his vast wisdom. I can't imagine what my son's life would be like today without Solomon's help.

God bless him!

Elaine and family

I first met Solomon J. Wickey in June, 1995. I had suffered for 15 years with heart blockage and about 8 years with Chronic Fatigue. I am a pastor and some of my people had gone to see Solomon with very favorable results. To be quite honest, I was very skeptical about going, but what did I have to lose?

At that point in time I had gone through four cardiac caths and three angioplasties. I couldn't walk the 250 feet to our mailbox without stopping. Just 45 days before my first visit to Solomon I had my 3rd angioplasty, yet the angina continued. According to the medical doctors, the next step was open heart surgery, or using a rotor to shave the blockage away.

When I sat down in front of Solomon, he looked into my eyes and said, "Oh my, you have a lot of blockage." He told me the extent of the blockage, as well as its location. I told him I was on medication, and he asked me when I started to feel worse. I told him it was when the doctor stopped me from jogging and put me on Mevacor and Procardia. He never once told me to stop taking them, it was up to me.

He told me it would be best if I just ate a good, well-balanced diet. At that time I was on a very strict low fat diet. I asked, "What about eggs? Can I eat them?" I will never forget his response. "Eat eggs. They are good for you as they are full of Lethicin and this is what actually softens plaque and helps clear it from your arteries."

He suggested several different herbs for me to take over the next three months, and told me that I might feel a little worse for a brief period, but then things would improve. On the way home we stopped to eat at Bob Evans and I enjoyed eggs for the first time in years.

Long story short, that was 1995, and Solomon was right. I am much improved...so much so that my doctor only wants to see me every two years. I did everything just as Solomon told me. I now walk 4 miles three times a week, including some steep hills, with little effort. Also, the day after I saw Solomon my Chronic Fatigue was gone after eight years of suffering.

I am grateful to God for the healing gift He has given to Solomon.

Kenneth L. Colvin, Waynesville, Ohio

I first heard of Solomon from my daughter who had an ailment that no test
or doctor could figure out. She went to him and he found a stone in her
spleen and dissolved it. She was relieved that he could help her and told her friends and family about him.

I have been to see Solomon on many occasions for various different reasons, but the most memorable one was when he gave me an herb to put on
the cancer on my leg. The doctors were wanting to operate with no guarantees.   The herb which I put on my leg, took the cancer away and left the good tissue unharmed. To this day, the cancer has never returned.

I am 76 years old and I make a trip from Texas every year to see Solomon
in Indiana just to fine tune things. The last time I went, my energy level was extremely low and now I feel better than I have in a long time.

Many people have been helped by Solomon Wickey, and we are extremely grateful for him and his abilities.

Sincerely,

Paul Minton

Shauna Brastock, D.C.
300 S. Madison Ave.
Greenwood, In. 46142
317) 882-3280

Note for Solomon's Touch

One of the greatest teachings ever is the Sermon on the Mount where Jesus describes to us how we should live our lives. Thats how I see you living your life, according to the Word. No man can save his brothers soul, or pay his brothers debt. We can and should help each other, but in the long run each person must do their own work.

Solomon, God have given you a special gift to help people. I thank you, for changing my life, mentally, physically, spirituallty, and lets not forget those wonderful emotions. You have touched my life in a very special way and I am forever grateful.

Dr. Shauna Brastock
Greenwood, In.